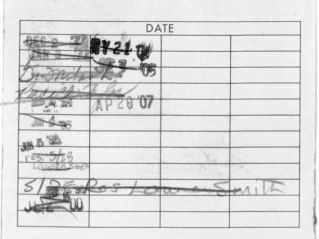

DATE			
AP 20 '07			

In 1848 the mania for gold swept through the United States and triggered a stampede for California. Lured by the dream of wealth, of something for nothing, the gold-seekers rushed west. They traveled 15,000 miles by ship around Cape Horn. They crossed the fever-ridden jungles and swamps of Panama. In huge numbers they made the 2,000 mile overland journey by covered wagon across the plains and mountains and deserts from Missouri to the Pacific Coast.

At their journey's end most of the forty-niners found, not fame and fortune, but loneliness, hardship, and back-breaking work. Many of them also found sickness, poverty, and death. Other people too paid a heavy price for this folly—Mexican-American and Chinese people were beaten and bullied, or driven from the mines, or killed; the California Indian population was decimated.

This is the story of the gold rush. It is a story of courage and heroism, cowardice and selfishness. Using contempo-rary accounts—the words of the forty-niners themselves—Professor Seidman casts a vivid light upon the human meaning of this extraordinary episode in American history.

THE FOOLS OF '49

The Living History Library
General Editor: John Anthony Scott

THE FOOLS OF '49

THE CALIFORNIA GOLD RUSH
1848-1856

Laurence I. Seidman

With maps, contemporary prints, photographs, and songs

ALFRED A. KNOPF: NEW YORK

979.4
Se-1

BJ533 10/77

THIS IS A BORZOI BOOK PUBLISHED BY ALFRED A. KNOPF, INC.

Copyright © 1976 by Laurence I. Seidman
All rights reserved under International and Pan-American Copyright Conventions.
Published in the United States by Alfred A. Knopf, Inc., New York,
and simultaneously in Canada by Random House of Canada Limited, Toronto.
Distributed by Random House, Inc., New York.

Library of Congress Cataloging in Publication Data
Seidman, Laurence Ivan, 1925-. The Fools of '49. (The Living History
Library.) Includes bibliographical references.
Summary: Traces the history of the gold rush in California
and discusses its impact on the development of that state.
1. California—Gold discoveries. 2. California—History—1848–1856.
3. Frontier and pioneer life—California. [1. California—Gold discoveries.
2. California—History—1848–1856] I. Title. F865.S44 979.4'04 74-164
Library of Congress Cataloging in Publication Data
ISBN 0-394-82685-X

Manufactured in the United States of America. 10 9 8 7 6 5 4 3 2 1

To Douglass, Karen, Larry, Leslie, Susan, and Samantha

CONTENTS

Introduction   3

THE FOOLS OF '49

INTRODUCTION

In January 1848 gold was discovered in California's Sacramento Valley. News of the discovery spread like lightning. People poured into California from all parts of the United States and from all over the world. They came by boat around Cape Horn, they came across the narrow waist of the Americas through the steamy swamps of Panama, and overland along the Oregon and California trails.

Those who came in the first years of the gold rush were mostly men lured by greed and the passion to get rich quick. They left behind their homes and families and staked all they had—including their very existence—on getting to California. Many did not live to see the land they dreamed of, for the hardships of the long trip were too much for them.

Those who did survive the journey found their way to the mining towns and camps and began to prospect for gold. Most of them were disappointed; only a few found either wealth or happiness. Many soon abandoned the gold fields and went on to other pursuits. They were

the founders of a new American state—California—
which had its origins in the gold rush and in the decima-
tion of the California Indians, which was an immediate
result of the white stampede to the Far West.

This is the story of that tragic experience.

GOLD IS DISCOVERED
IN CALIFORNIA

"Gold! Gold! Gold from the American River!" yelled a man, rushing up and down the streets of San Francisco, waving a bottle of gold dust in one hand and his hat in the other.

Sam Brannan, a Mormon elder, storekeeper, and real estate speculator, had just returned from the new gold find up beyond Sutter's Fort on the American River. People swarmed out into the streets and gathered about him, examining the dust in the bottle, listening, talking, gesturing, arguing. It was May 12, 1848.

An electric current swept through the town. People lost their reason. Gold was to be had for the taking. Anyone, everyone, could become rich. You could pick up nuggets with your bare hands, or dig them out of the rocks with a pocket knife.

People left for the diggings by foot, horse, mule and wagon, primitive stagecoach, or on any type of boat that would float up the Sacramento River. Shopkeepers put up their shutters, real estate men disposed of their holdings, workers quit their jobs, houses were left vacant. Stores were rummaged for pickaxes, hoes, bottles, vials, snuffboxes, and brass tubes, the latter for holding the gold.

Merchants hung out signs that said: *Gone to the Diggings. Help yourself. Put your money in the cash drawer and take your own change.*

Two months earlier, the United States had taken over California from Mexico. In that time San Francisco had become a growing town; scores of buildings had been started. But now, complained Edwin Kimble, editor of the San Francisco *Star*:

Stores are closed and places of business vacated, a large number of houses tenantless, various kinds of mechanical labor suspended or given up entirely, and nowhere the pleasant hum of industry salutes the ear as of late; but as if a curse had arrested our onward course of enterprise, everything wears a desolate and sombre look; everywhere all is dull, monotonous, dead.

San Francisco came to look like a ghost town. In vain did Kimble beg: "Pay up before you go—everybody knows where. Pay the printer if you please."

Nobody pleased. The *Star* and its rival, the *Californian*, suspended publication; there were no subscribers left. Kimble took leave of his readers on June 14 with these pensive words:

The whole country from San Francisco to Los Angeles and from the seashore to the base of the Sierra Nevada resounds to the sordid cry of gold! Gold! GOLD!!! My paper cannot be printed by magic and as everybody is deserting me, paper and press must stop together.

The town council ceased to meet; all the councilors

had gone "you know where." Churches closed their doors, their congregations having disappeared into the hills.

Deserted by their crews, boats lay idle in San Francisco Bay. A Peruvian ship put in, and not a soul came down from the town to greet her. Her captain, fearful of a plague, went ashore and hailed the first person he saw, a Mexican.

"What's the matter here?" he asked.

"Everybody has gone into the north, señor, where there are valleys and mountains of gold."

"What!"

Within an hour, the ship was deserted by its crew.

The news spread like wildfire through the rest of California. Farmers left their wheat standing in the fields; mills stopped running. One man received a letter from his two brothers, already in the gold fields: "Burn your livery barn, if you can't dispose of it otherwise, but come at once!" And away he went.

One American who had a ringside seat for the gold rush was the Reverend Walter Colton. Colton had been a chaplain in the United States Navy and had arrived in California aboard the U.S.S. *Congress* in 1846. When the American flag was raised at Monterey and San Francisco on July 10, 1846, Colton was appointed mayor of Monterey, a position he held for three years. In 1850 he published a book about his experiences titled *Three Years in California*. The Reverend Mr. Colton tells how the gold fever spread:

Tuesday, July 18. Another bag of gold from the mines and another spasm in the community. It was brought down by a sailor from Yuba river, and contains a hundred and thirty-six ounces. It is the most beautiful gold that has appeared in the market; it looks like the yellow scales of the dolphin, passing through his rainbow hues at death. My carpenters, at work on the schoolhouse, on seeing it, threw down their saws and planes, shouldered their picks, and are off for the Yuba. Three seamen ran from the Warren, forfeiting their four years' pay; and a whole platoon of soldiers from the fort left only their colors behind.

Criminals broke their paroles and headed for the fields; sheriffs and jailors followed after, not to catch them, but to reach the fields first. At San Jose, a constable had ten prisoners in his jail, two of them murderers. There was nobody to leave them with, so he marched them on the road before him, taking them into the fields to work in the diggings for him. He made a fortune from their labor until they decided to go prospecting for themselves.

Even the servants were infected, wrote Colton in despair, as household help disappeared.

Saturday, July 15. The gold fever has reached every servant in Monterey; none are to be trusted in their engagement beyond a week. Gen. Mason, Lieut. Lauman, and myself, form a mess; we have a house, and all the table furniture and culinary apparatus requisite; but our servants have run. This morning, for the fortieth time, we had to take to the kitchen, and cook our own breakfast. A general of the United States Army, the commander of a man-of-war, and the Alcalde of Monterey, in a smoking kitchen, grinding coffee, toasting a herring, and peeling onions! These gold mines are going to upset all the domestic arrangements of society.

The blacksmith dropped his hammer, the baker his loaf, the dentist his drill, the judge his gavel. Soldiers and sailors were infected by the gold fever, too. Some forty men of Company C, stationed at Sonora, laid down their arms and marched off to the gold region. Warrants were issued for the apprehension of deserters, but to no avail. There was no one to serve them. "I don't blame the fellow a whit," said Colton, talking of a soldier's desertion. "Seven dollars a month, while others are making two or three hundred a day! That is too much for human nature to stand."

Colonel Richard B. Mason, military governor of California, issued a proclamation appealing to civilians to turn in deserters. Dated July 25, 1848, at Monterey, California, it read:

Persons employed at the mines are reminded that up to this time they have enjoyed the high privilege of digging gold on government land without charge and without hinderance. In return for this privilege they are bound to assist in apprehending deserters and of giving notice to the nearest military officer where they are concealed.

A dragoon force will soon be at the mining district and will traverse it in every direction, to arrest deserters from the army and navy and to apprehend such citizens as harbor or employ them.

Despite Colonel Mason's appeal, desertions continued, and no force of dragoons ever appeared at the mines.

The news flowed north into Oregon and Canada; south to Mexico and South America; across the Pacific to Honolulu, Australia, and the Far East. People came in droves. Indians, Hawaiians, Chileans, Argentinians, Brazilians, Colombians, Australians, Chinese, and Japanese mixed with Mexicans, Spaniards, and North Americans. People from every walk of life rubbed shoulders: soldiers, sailors, gentlemen, pimps, dentists, farmers, prostitutes, gamblers, criminals, sheriffs, clerks, lawyers, merchants, doctors, parsons, ranchers, cardsharps, saloonkeepers, drunkards, and mayors.

Within three months, reported Hubert Bancroft, the famous Californian historian, four thousand men were at work in the diggings, of whom over half were Indians. New discoveries were made almost every day:

The world came flocking in. The region round Marshall's mill soon swarmed with gold seekers. Two thousand diggers were at work there with knives, picks, shovels, sticks, tin pans, wooden bowls, willow baskets and cradles, picking crevices, scraping rocky beds, riddling gravely sand and washing dirt for the metal. Shortly after there were some four thousand upon the ground, if we include natives who were mostly employed by white men. It was then discovered that all about in the vicinity of Marshall's mill gold abounded. New discoveries followed in quick succession, each adding fuel to the flame. Every gulch and ravine was prospected. Finally, the fact became apparent that all along the base of the Sierra, from one end of the great valley of California to the other, almost every rivulet, gulch and canyon was rich in gold.

California talked gold, thought gold, slept gold, and dreamed gold—pounds of it, sacks of it, barrels of it, bushels of it, wagons of it. And all of it to be picked up or dug out without cost as fast as a man could work. There was enough for everybody. It was impossible not to become rich.

A vast sea of humanity swarmed into the gold fields. Colton describes their presence:

Wednesday, Nov. 8. Some fifty thousand persons are drifting up and down these slopes of the great Sierra, of every hue, language and clime, tumultuous and confused as a flock of wild geese. All are in quest of gold; and with eyes dilated to the circle of the moon, rush this way and that, as some new discovery or fictious tale of success may suggest. Some are with tents, and some without; some have provisions and some are on their last ration; some are carrying crowbars; some pickaxes and spades; some wash-bowls and cradles; some hammers and drills, and powder enough to blow up the rock of Gibraltar.

It all started at Sutter's sawmill, near the south fork of the American River, forty miles from Sutter's Fort and from where the American emptied into the Sacramento River. The sawmill was located in the Coloma Valley, which means "beautiful valley" in the Indian language. On January 24, 1848, James Marshall was supervising some Mormon workmen who were building a sawmill for Captain John Augustus Sutter. Marshall's eye was caught by something yellow glittering in the bottom of the millrace, the channel of water which ran under the mill wheel. He scooped up some yellow flakes of soft material. Hammering and biting it, Marshall decided that it might be gold.

Carrying the yellow metal in the crown of his hat, Marshall walked up to the workmen, halted, gazed from one man to another, and said solemnly: "Boys, I have got her now. I believe I've found gold."

Most of the men thought Marshall was crazy. Gold in a millrace? But together with Marshall they compared it with a five-dollar goldpiece, heated it in a fire, and tested it in a pot full of boiling lye. By golly, maybe it *was* gold.

Excited, Marshall rode down to the fort to show his find to Captain Sutter. Originally from Switzerland, where he had been a storekeeper, Sutter had done poorly there. Finally he abandoned both his debtors and his family and came to America and became a citizen. He had moved to California in July 1839 and secured a large grant of land from the Mexican government. Here he had built Sutter's Fort, on the site of the present city of Sacramento. Building a tannery and raising grain and cattle, he sold supplies of flour, beef, and leather to the incoming settlers. He had prospered and was a rich and influential man. He owned 12,000 cattle, 2,000 horses and mules, over 10,000 sheep, and 1,000 hogs. In his employ were more than a thousand people—Americans, Mormons, Mexicans, and Indians.

In the Sacramento Valley lumber was scarce and in demand. Sutter decided to build a sawmill in the foothills of the mountains. He hired a moody, thirty-five-year-old wagonmaker and carpenter from New Jersey, James Wilson Marshall, to find a good site for the sawmill, build it, and run it for Sutter. This was the man who burst into Sutter's private office on the night of February 2, 1848.

Marshall asked Sutter to make sure they were alone and even to lock the door.

Sutter's Fort, 1847

James Marshall

Sutter's Mill

Laboring under great excitement, with haggard eyes, weary look and mud-spattered clothes, which raised the question of sanity in Sutter's mind, he drew from his saddle-bags a buckskin pouch and poured out on the table about an ounce of coarse lumps of metal. He said, "These are gold."

Sutter and Marshall tested the yellow material further. They weighed it on a scale, and poured some nitric acid on the flakes and grains. Taking down a volume of the *American Encyclopedia*, Sutter read the long article about gold. The material that Marshall had found met all tests. It was gold all right.

Sutter was quite concerned. If word got out about the gold, his workers would leave him, and his sawmill would never be finished. A lot of crazy gold-seekers would overrun his land. Sutter went up to the sawmill and gathered the Mormon and Indian workers around him. He got them to agree to keep the news of the gold a secret for the next six weeks so that they could finish the mill. All the men agreed, but a secret is not so easily kept.

A Greek myth recounts the tale of King Midas of Phrygia, whose ears were changed by the god Apollo into the ears of an ass. To hide his disfigurement the king always wore a hat. Only his servant knew the king's secret, and he was sworn never to tell it to anyone, upon penalty of death. For a while the servant kept the secret; still, it was the kind of secret you had to tell someone or burst. Finally, the servant dug a hole in the ground and whispered into it, "King Midas has the ears of an ass! King Midas has the ears of an ass!" But the secret was so terrible that the earth told it to the reeds, and the reeds whispered it to the breeze, and the breeze carried it all over the world: "King Midas has the ears of an ass! King Midas has the ears of an ass!"

It was the same way with the gold. Sutter himself was able to keep it to himself for only ten days before he simply had to write about it to an old Mexican friend. Then a teamster who brought supplies to the site of the sawmill learned about the gold. Sworn to secrecy, he stopped at a saloon for a drink and blurted out the news, showing the gold dust he had received as pay for his supplies. And while the Mormon workers continued building the mill, they spent every spare moment out hunting for gold. Once the mill was finished, all of Sutter's workers went off gold mining on their own. No one was left to tan the hides or thresh the wheat or run the sawmill.

By May, all normal life at Sutter's Fort ceased. It became a stopping place for gold-seekers bound for the diggings. Every day new gold fields were discovered, and more and more people poured in. Coloma became the center of the upper mines. Houses went up by the hundreds, and it grew into a thriving city. Sutter had sold his half interest in the sawmill, which was now busy turning out lumber for new buildings and stores.

Sutter's Fort became the center of the lower mines; and at first, Sutter prospered. He sold supplies as fast as he could unpack them. Every building he owned was rented at exorbitant prices to merchants and store-keepers. Money lost all value as the gold-seekers were willing to pay any price for supplies. Those who found gold spent it as if it were sand; they felt they could always get more.

Prices soared. Flour sold at $800 a barrel, sugar at $400. Eggs were $3 apiece, and a pound of bread cost $2. Shovels sold for $10, $20, and even $100. Merchants averaged sales of $2,000 to $3,000 a day and made about 300 percent on their cost. Wages were unbelievable: clerks got at least $300 a month and hotel cooks $200.

Later, Sutter was ruined. As the forty-niners flooded the area, they paid no attention to Sutter's land claims. They squatted and paid him nothing. He lost everything and died a bitter and disappointed man. Marshall, too, lost all he had and died penniless.

The activity and excitement at the fort were described by Heinrich Leinhard, Sutter's Swiss gardener, who noted in his journal:

Exciting rumors began to spread with the rapidity of a great epidemic. Everyone was infected and as it spread, peace and quiet vanished. To all appearances men seemed to have gone insane, or to have suddenly lost some of their five senses; they were apparently living in a dream. Each man had to stop and ask himself: "Am I mad? Is all this real? Is what I see with my own eyes actually gold or is it merely my imagination? Is it a chimera? Am I delirious?"

At first the news spread slowly in California. People had heard so many rumors of gold being discovered that no one could believe it when it finally happened. The first news of the strike appeared in the San Francisco *Californian* on March 15, 1848, in a small article on the second page, at the bottom of the third column:

Gold Mine Found. In the newly made raceway of the Saw Mill recently erected by Captain Sutter on the American fork, gold has been found in considerable quantities. One person brought thirty dollars worth to New Helvetia, gathered there in a short time. California, no doubt, is rich in mineral wealth, great chance here for scientific capitalists. Gold has been found in almost every part of the country.

But with Sam Brannan's dramatic announcement in San Francisco, and with the gold dust as proof, the people became electrified. The gold rush was on. *California* became a word known throughout the world—and the way of life that had existed there for centuries was never to be the same again.

California Boy

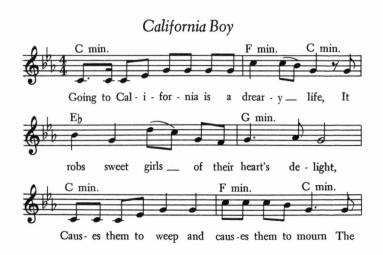

Going to Cal - i - for - nia is a drear - y — life, It
robs sweet girls — of their heart's de - light,
Caus - es them to weep and caus - es them to mourn The

loss of a true love — nev-er to re-turn.

Going to California is a dreary life,
It robs sweet girls of their heart's delight,
Causes them to weep and causes them to mourn
The loss of a true love never to return.

"Captain, oh captain, bring me a boat
That I may on the ocean float;
I'll hail each vessel passing by
And there I'll enquire for my California boy."

"Black is the color of my true love's hair!
His cheeks resemble the roses fair.
His eyes are black, his lips like wine,
Ten thousand thousand times they have met with mine."

"Dig my grave both wide and deep,
Put marble stones at my head and feet;
And on my breast a turtle dove
To show to the world that I died for love."

THE NEWS SPREADS TO THE EAST

On June 1, 1848, Thomas C. Larkin, then the United States consul of northern California, sat at his desk in San Francisco. He was writing a letter to James Buchanan, the secretary of state in far-off Washington, D.C., who would later become the nation's fifteenth President.

Sir: I have to report to the State Department one of the most astonishing experiences and state of affairs now existing in this country that perhaps has ever been brought to the notice of this government.

Gold had been discovered, he told Buchanan. Larkin had seen it and talked to the men who had dug it up. Why, with a shovel and a bowl, a man could make a fortune. The whole of California was going mad.

Another visitor to the gold fields, Colonel Mason, wrote much the same story to the adjutant general of the United States in Washington, D.C. He reported that merchants were paying Sutter rents of $100 a month for a single room. A two-story house at Sutter's Fort rented as a hotel for $500 a month. He added that "no officer can now live in California on his pay; money has so little value."

Colonel Mason sent a young officer, Lieutenant Loeser,

to carry dispatches, maps, and a tea caddy containing 230 ounces of gold purchased at San Francisco to the adjutant general. Lieutenant Loeser was to travel to Panama, cross the Isthmus, and continue by boat.

Lieutenant Loeser was beaten to Washington by the Navy. Lieutenant Edward Fitzgerald Beale, with gold samples and dispatches of its discovery, had crossed Mexico on horseback. Disguised as a poor Mexican, but carrying four navy revolvers and a butcher knife, Lieutenant Beale was chased by bandits and had to travel day and night to outride them. Arriving in Washington in the middle of September, he appeared before the United States Senate. The news of the discovery of gold made the front pages of newspapers in the East. The Baltimore *Sun*'s headline on September 20 proclaimed: *Rich Gold Fields Have Been Discovered in California!* The Washington, D.C., *National Intelligencer* read: *Lt. Beale Appears Before the Senate* and then published Beale's own story of his dramatic trip.

Crowds followed Beale about the streets and even into his hotel, begging to see and feel the gold. Half the gold that Beale had brought was put on view in the Patents Office in Washington. The other half, the young lieutenant had made into an engagement ring for the girl he was to marry.

The morning edition of the New York *Herald* of Thursday, September 21, 1848, gave this "Intelligence by the Mails" from Washington, September 19:

All Washington is in a ferment with the news of the immense bed of gold, which, it is said, has been discovered in California. Nothing else is talked about. Democrats, Whigs, free soil men, hunkers, barnburners, abolitionists, all, all are engrossed by the wonderful intelligence. The real El Dorado has at length been discovered, and hereafter let not cynics doubt that such a place exists.

At the end of November, Lieutenant Loeser arrived in Washington with his tea caddy and his dispatches. The gold he brought was tested in the Philadelphia Mint and pronounced to be of the highest standards. Colonel Mason's reports and maps were incorporated in President Polk's annual message to Congress on December 5, 1848. His words were widely reported in newspapers throughout the country:

The accounts of the abundance of gold in that territory are of such an extraordinary character as would scarcely command belief were they not corroborated by the authentic reports of officers in the public service who have visited the mineral district, and derived the facts which they detail from personal observation.

The President quoted Mason's description of his visit to Weber's Creek at Placerville.

A small gutter not more than 100 yards long, but four feet wide and two or three feet deep, was pointed out to me as the one where two men, William Daly and Perry McCoon, had a short time before, obtained in seven days $17,000 worth of gold. Captain Weber informed me, that he knew that these two men had employed four white men and one hundred Indians, and that at the end of one week's work, they paid off their party and left with $10,000 worth of this gold. Another small ravine was shown to me from which had been taken $12,000 worth of gold. Hundreds of similar ravines, to all appearances, are as yet untouched.

These confirmations touched off the gold mania in the East. All over the eastern half of the country, newspapers added flames to the excitement. Said Horace Greeley in his New York *Tribune*: "It is coming—nay at hand, there is no doubt of it. We are on the very brink of the Age of Gold!"

Newspapers teemed with the wildest kinds of stories and letters from California.

Any able bodied man, with a simple shovel and sieve, can procure about fifty dollars worth of gold per day. In some cases, however, it is said that persons have collected as much as a pound of gold in a single day valued at the current rates there at over two hundred dollars.

The precious metal which is found in the gold region is said to be so plentiful, that it lies mingled with the sand upon the surface of the plains and in the beds of rivers.

It appears in the form of dust and small leaves, and during bright sunshiny days, glitters for miles around, so as almost to dazzle and blind the eyes.

No story was too absurd or too extravagant to be believed. Nothing was questioned. There were mountains of pure gold. Why, just by brushing the dirt from the seams of your coat, you would get gold. Nuggets were being found that were the size of large potatoes. A man wrote a book saying that in ten days he had picked up gold worth over $50,000.

Letters from gold miners on the spot to relatives, friends, and newspapers back home helped inflame the fever. Wrote one:

My little girls can make from 5 to 25 dollars per day washing gold in pans. My average income this winter will be about $150 per day and if I should strike a good lead it will be a great deal more.

Another Californian wrote:

I am writing at the table of a gentleman worth fifty thousand dollars, who came out as a private soldier in Stevenson's regiment from New York. Everyone who has been to the mines says that the gold is inexhaustible. ... There is a mountain of silver about ninety miles east of this, which yields ninety per cent, but nothing short of gold can tempt the miner.

Gold fever swept the country. Everywhere the talk was of going to California and of gold. New York City, the financial and commercial center of the country, was a madhouse. Businesses were sold at a fraction of their value. Lawyers left their clients, students the universities, workers their jobs, teachers their classes. Gold fever, California fever, yellow fever, California mania, gold mania—call it what you will. Nothing mattered except to get to California.

Pawnshops were kept busy as people pawned their jewelry, silverware, watches, and other possessions for passage money to California. Use your savings; beg or borrow for the ship's fare. Mortgage your house, farm, or business, your wife or children. Within a month after arriving in the diggings, you will be so rich that you will be able to buy back everything a dozen times over.

At the end of January, the New York *Tribune* declared:

A resident of New York, coming back after a three months' absence, would wonder at the word "California" seen everywhere in glaring letters and at the column of

"California News" a painting by
William Sidney Mount, 1850

vessels advertised in the papers, about to sail for San Francisco. He would be puzzled at seeing a new class of men in the streets, in a peculiar costume—broad, felt hats of a reddish brown hue, loose, rough coats reaching to the knees, and high boots. Californians throng the streets; several of the hotels are almost filled with them, and though large numbers leave every day, there is no apparent diminution of their numbers. Even those who have watched the gradual progress of the excitement are astonished at its extent and intensity. The ordinary course of business seems for the time to be changed; bakers keep their ovens hot day and night, turning out immense quantities of ship bread, without supplying the demand; the provision stores of all kinds are besieged by orders. Manufacturers of rubber goods, rifles, pistols, bowie knives, etc., can scarcely supply the demand.

Philadelphia, Boston, Baltimore, New Orleans—every port and city was as infected by the fever as New York. In the interior of the country the cities along the Mississippi Valley, especially St. Louis, were just as feverish.

The rest of the world went mad too. In Europe, 1848 had been a year of revolution, and the Continent had heaved from center to circumference. France had banished her king and proclaimed the equality and brotherhood of man. Popular uprisings had spread to other states, and Prince Metternich, leader of the great Austrian Empire, was overthrown. Political disturbances had occurred in Bohemia, Hungary, and the Italian states. Germany, Sweden, Denmark, Holland, and the British Isles had all been shaken.

But the popular revolts for political and economic

freedom were put down. Reaction and oppression returned to rule Europe. Discontented and uneasy, Europeans responded to the news of the California gold rush with enthusiasm and vigor. The New World would remedy conditions, bring prosperity and freedom from the bad times they were enduring. Although little was known about this far-off land, tales circulated that California was the land of enchantment, where it was always either spring or summer. Here they would find riches that would change their destinies. Thousands of English, Irish, Spanish, Dutch, French, and German people rushed to emigrate to America—to share in the gold rush. In France, lotteries were held, with the winners given a free trip to the gold mines. "Every newspaper is filled with invitations for merchandise, capital and emigrants to be dispatched to that region," wrote a correspondent. French investment companies were formed, calling themselves The Transatlantic Company, The Eldorado, The Golden Harvest, The Golden Hive, and The French and American Company of San Francisco.

Gold in California! Rich and poor, old and young, blind and maimed started for the diggings. Ministers, bankers, laymen—the godly, the flesh and the devil—all joined in the chase for riches. Gold was the fox, the world the hounds, and all in full cry.

Soon the air was filled with would-be miners singing a popular folk song of the day. Set to the tune of Stephen Foster's "Camptown Races," the words described the boundless enthusiasm of the gold-seekers. It was entitled "Sacramento," or "The Banks of Sacramento."

Banks of the Sacramento

Cal - i - for- ny - o,   There's plen- ty of gold so
I've been told On the banks of the Sac - ra - men - to.

A bully ship and a bully crew
    Dooda, dooda,
A bully mate and a captain too,
    Dooda dooda day.

CHORUS:

Then blow ye winds hi-oh
For Californyo
There's plenty of gold so I've been told
On the banks of the Sacramento.

Oh around Cape Horn we're bound to go,
    Dooda, dooda,
Around Cape Horn through the sleet and snow,
    Dooda, dooda day.

CHORUS

Oh around Cape Horn in the month of May,
    Dooda, dooda,
Oh around Cape Horn is a very long way,
    Dooda, dooda day.

CHORUS

Ninety days to Frisco Bay,
    Dooda, dooda
Ninety days is damn good pay,
    Dooda, dooda day.

CHORUS

I wish to God I'd never been born,
    Dooda, dooda,
To go a-sailin' round Cape Horn,
    Dooda, dooda day.

CHORUS

To the Sacramento we're bound away,
    Dooda, dooda,
To the Sacramento's a hell of a way,
    Dooda, dooda day.

CHORUS

Later, when the forty-niners returned to their homes, other verses, satiric and bitter, were sung to the tune. And the chorus was changed to one closer to the truth:

> Then blow ye winds, hi-oh! for Californyo!
> There's plenty of stones and dead men's bones
> On the banks of the Sac-ra-men-to.

What was the quickest way to get to the gold fields? Young men from the Atlantic seaport cities, familiar with the ocean, favored going by ship. You had your choice of two water routes, and both were open all year.

By the first route, you could sail around South America by way of Cape Horn to San Francisco. This entailed a journey of 17,000 miles and could take from four to nine months, depending upon the ship and the weather. Your second choice was to sail to Panama, leave the ship, then strike out overland and cross the isthmus by foot, canoe, and muleback. Reaching the Pacific, you caught another boat up to San Francisco. This was a shorter route and therefore supposedly faster. But both routes had their advocates.

The demand for passage by ship was so heavy that passenger lists in Philadelphia, New York, Boston, and Baltimore were filled almost the same day they were opened. There were not enough ships to take all who wished to go. Many lines withdrew their ships from their regular runs and put them on the route around Cape Horn. Almost the entire New England whaling fleet was converted to carrying passengers instead of oil. Money seemed to be no object, and shipowners raised their rates as high as they dared. Still the stream of prospective gold diggers flowed aboard.

Every ship, no matter how old or battered or unseaworthy, was pressed into service. Overhauled, repainted, repatched, and advertised as being safe, the ships were filled to the gunwales with passengers desperate to get to the gold fields. No one seemed to care about comfort or safety, just as long as the vessel floated. Captains and crews were selected haphazardly. Often they were inexperienced and incompetent. Undermanned and overcrowded ships were sailing on one of the most strenuous sea routes in the world. No matter, just as long as you got aboard. These would-be forty-niners, their heads filled with visions of gold, had complete confidence in their ability to survive the long voyage and arrive in time to make their pile. Over five hundred ships left Atlantic and Gulf ports for California during 1849.

It was a madness, a circus, a spectacle such as was never witnessed before. Dr. Stillman, a physician who was himself one of the argonauts leaving from New York by ship for the gold fields, summed it up by saying: "Never since the Crusades was such a movement known. Not a family but had one or two or more representatives gone or preparing to go."

A few voices were raised against the mass hysteria and warned about the dangers and hardships of the trip, the lack of shelter and food in the diggings, the hard work involved, the vices that would be aroused. These were pointed out—plus the fact that only merchants and gamblers would benefit and that misery and suffering would be the lot of the rest.

In words that were to prove all too true, B. P. Goodwin, an Englishman, wrote in *The People's Journal*:

That it will be disastrous to many of those who engage

A cartoonist's interpretation of
"Anything that would float"

personally in this adventure is in accordance with all the experiences of history on similar occasions. Some who go away will leave behind them families who will starve to death in their absence; others will fall victims to the diseases of unfriendly climates; many will not be successful for want of instruments and assistance when they arrive there, or will perish for the want of shelter and food; such as may be successful, elated by sudden acquisition, will abandon themselves to gaming, drinking and other vices; others again, will squander what they procure in insane schemes and speculations; while only a few, and these principally merchants already rich, will profit greatly by the event.

One must tremble when he thinks of the vast amount of private misery which will be necessarily engendered by the mania for gold. What disappointments, what positive sufferings, what anguish of mind and broken hearts!

Immense speculations and immense losses are inevitable. People will go mad with the imagination of boundless wealth which is about to flow in upon them in streams; they will risk their all in desperate adventures; extravagant and ruinous habits will take the place of prudent economy.

But who would listen when fortune was waiting? Everyone was going, so surely it must all be true. To be "off to California" made you one of the community's farsighted young men. It placed you a peg above the ordinary; it proved you had enterprise and vision.

Many young men had returned from the Mexican War and found it hard to settle down into the placid life they had lived before. They were restless and eager

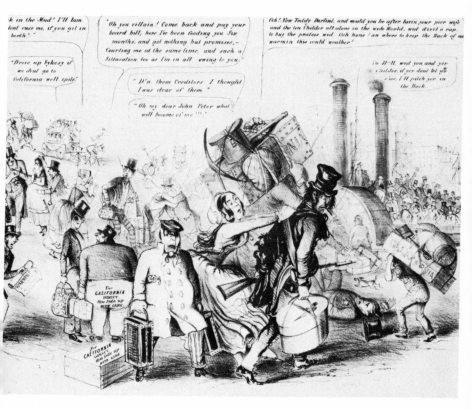

Off for California, 1849 cartoon

for adventure. Western travel—to see the prairies, the buffalo, and Indians; to cross the mountains and deserts; or to sail the seas—promised a welcome relief from the humdrum routine of their lives. California offered them excitement—and the promise of wealth without hard work.

The news of the gold rush sounded like a great giveaway. For the first time in American history, Dame Fortune held out the promise of something for nothing to thousands who had little hope of improving their standing in the normal course of their lives. Men who had never dreamed of anything beyond a bare subsistence were dazzled by the gleam and glitter of gold. It was a fairy tale come true. There really was a pot of gold at the end of the rainbow, and it was there for the taking. And every man, regardless of education, position, or wealth, had an equal chance. No matter what your status in life had been before, you had a chance to make your fortune and live in luxury for the rest of your life.

The dream of the Jacksonian Americans was interwoven with the frontier—a dream of land, independence, self-reliance, and human equality. It was also interwoven with the ideas of abundance and of the freedom that comes from being the possessor of property, emancipated from poverty and want. By 1849, all the facets of the dream were symbolized by gold. Men abandoned everything in their rush to get to the diggings.

To the west seemed to lie more fertile fields and a more satisfactory life. Many men, eager to get a new start, abandoned failing businesses, poor farms, or stale occupations. They needed only the slightest excuse to head westward.

The San Francisco *Pacific News* quoted an article from the London *Atheneum* of September 1849 describing the gypsylike qualities of the "Universal Yankee Nation."

No land is too far, no nook too stark for their researches. If a taste for copper should lead you to the bottom of a Cornish mine, there will be found one of the sovereigns of the Republic; should a good morning tempt you to the top of the grand pyramid, there you will find Cousin Jonathan astride the apex. Should the northwest passage ever be discovered, a Yankee will probably be found there on a stranded iceberg.

"What do I consider the boundary of my country, sir?" exclaimed a Kentuckian. "Why, sir, on the east we are bounded by the rising sun, and on the north by the aurora borealis; on the west by the procession of the equinoxes and on the south by the day of judgement."

It was estimated that a forty-niner needed a minimum of $750 in order to pay his fare; buy clothing, supplies, and food; and have some capital left when he reached the gold fields. This was a very large sum of money for these times, yet many of the young forty-niners were able to raise it. Frequently it was loaned to them by the older, wealthier citizens of their towns, who could not make the hazardous voyage themselves. They were willing to finance a young prospector in exchange for a share of the wealth the argonaut would surely find in the diggings. Neither borrower nor lender had the least doubt that riches would be found and the loan repaid.

In the early rush to California, most of the gold-seekers traveling by ship were men. Few women undertook the long, hazardous trip in 1849, when conditions aboard vessels were crowded and primitive. The majority of the forty-niners did not plan to stay in California. They were going there to make their fortunes; they meant to return east as quickly as possible. Later, many of them decided to stay in the new country and sent for their wives and families.

By the mid-1850s, better ship accommodations and faster voyages were inducing more women to make the trip. The womanless towns of the California mining regions attracted young women looking for marriage and companionship. Often the miners and the women had corresponded; after two or three letters, the lonely forty-niner would propose and send for his bride-to-be to come out and join him in California.

One enterprising woman, Mrs. Eliza Woodson Farnham, a former matron at Sing Sing Prison, came to Boston planning to lead a band of marriageable women to San Francisco. Chartering a vessel, the *Angelique*, she set passage for young females at $200. She pointed out that in California, jobs as waitresses, laundresses, clerks, bookkeepers, and nurses were plentiful at lucrative wages. But most important, there were lots of eligible, woman-hungry gold miners, who would be uplifted and reformed by the presence of decent women in California society. On April 12, 1850, the New York *Tribune* saluted Mrs. Farnham and her plan; but alas, she was unsuccessful. The *Angelique* sailed in June, carrying only Mrs. Farnham and three other women, two of them widows, along with fifteen male passengers.

A majority of the emigrants, especially those from New England, banded together into companies and traveled westward in groups. Frequently they were organized on a military basis, and uniforms were worn by their members. Many were members of joint stock companies. A share entitled a stockholder to his transportation and a part of the profits. Most of these companies had a written constitution, a common treasury, elected officers, and fixed dues. Every matter of importance was put to a vote, each man having an equal voice.

Frequently these companies also carried merchandise to sell in California. Thus they expected to make a profit not only through mining, but also through trading. Unfortunately, they often brought the wrong merchandise, goods that were either not in demand or were already overstocked in California. It was hard for them to know in advance what was needed. Often, several vessels would arrive in San Francisco on the same day, and there would be a glut of merchandise. Frequently the companies bringing merchandise suffered losses rather than making profits. Much of the goods they carried was poorly packed and was damaged and spoiled by the sea air and moisture of the long voyage.

Some companies chartered their own boats to take them to California. The oldest and slowest vessels were purchased because they were the cheapest. Few companies could afford to charter the fastest brigs or clippers. The clippers, "Greyhounds of the Sea," were produced to meet the demand and need for speed to California at any price. Passenger room on the clippers was limited and fares were high; they mainly carried merchandise requested by California merchants. Cargo rates for these goods shot up so phenomenally that many of the clippers paid for themselves on their first round trip to San Francisco.

FOR
CALIFORNIA!
Mutual Protection
Trading & Mining Co.

Having purchased the splendid, Coppered and very fast Sailing

Barque EMMA ISIDORA,

Will leave about the 15th of February. This vessel will be fitted in the very best manner and is one of the fastest sailing vessels that goes from this port.

Each member pays 300 dollars and is entitled to an equal proportion of all profits made by the company either at mining or trading, and holds an equal share of all the property belonging to the company. Experienced men well acquainted with the coast and climate are already engaged as officers of the Company. A rare chance is offered to any wishing a safe investment, good home and Large profits.

This Company is limited to 60 and any wishing to improve this opportunity must make immediate application.

An Experienced Physician will go with the company.

For Freight or Passage apply to 23 State Street, corner of Devonshire, where the list of Passengers may be seen.

JAMES H. PRINCE, Agent,
23 State Street, corner of Devonshire St., Boston.

For further Particulars, see the Constitution.

Propeller Power Presses,
142 Washington St., Boston.

Poster advertising one of the trading
and mining companies

The gold rush marked the golden age of the great Yankee clipper ships, but most forty-niners saw them only at sea, as they outdistanced their own slower ships and sped away over the horizon. Clipper ships were built in great profusion in the 1850s. But in the next decade the rush to the gold fields subsided, and faced with the competition of the railroads and the problems brought on by the Civil War, the clippers often had trouble finding cargoes to fill their holds.

Shipowners and shipbuilders were not the only ones to profit from gold mania. Manufacturers and merchants throughout the country flooded the market with all kinds of equipment and supplies that any self-respecting gold miner had to have to be assured of being successful. The greenhorn miner, not wishing to be unprepared, was as anxious to buy as the merchants were to sell. Anything marked "miners' supplies," or that carried the word "California," was gobbled up by the eager hordes. Store windows were filled with "gold nuggets" surrounded by articles essential to the gold-seekers. Banners advertising California merchandise were displayed throughout the town, draped over stores, hotels, saloons, outfitters, and suppliers.

Newspaper columns bulged with advertisements directed to the forty-niners.

FOR CALIFORNIA. *The subscriber continues to supply individuals, companies and the trade with Gold Sifters and Washers, Miners' and Gold Picks, Pickaxes, Shovels, Spades, Hoes, Axes and Hatchets, Knives and Forks, Hunters' Knives, Dirks and Bowie Knives, Guns, Rifles, Carbines, Pistols & c. Percussion Caps, Sand Crucibles, Black Lead, Pots, Mortars and Pestles, Jewelers' & Smiths'*

Forges, Ingots for running Gold and Tests for Gold; Powder, Shot, Pig and Bar Lead, Tents, Hammocks & c. comprising a general assortment of Hardware, Cutlery Edge Tools & c. particularly adapted to the California market and the trade in general.

Shovels with depressions in their scoops to hold the gold while you washed the dirt away, blankets, canteens, clothing, "preserved foods," testing kits for gold, quick medicines, waterproof tents, money belts to store the gold, waterproof matches, sheet-iron collapsible houses that could be easily put together and taken down, gold-washing machines and gold-finding machines, and a thousand other items and new inventions were offered to the prospective gold-seeker.

For those going by way of Panama, through the jungle and across the isthmus, manufacturers advertised "all manner of absurd and useless articles." J. D. Borthwick, a forty-niner who traveled the Panama route, remarked how the gold-seekers were burdened down with equipment "they were told were indispensable to crossing the Isthmus":

Some were equipped with pots, pans, kettles, dining-cups, knives, and forks, spoons, pocket-filters (for they had been told that the water on the Isthmus was very dirty), India-rubber contrivances, which an ingenious man with a powerful imagination and strong lungs could blow up and convert into a bed, a boat or a tent—bottles of "cholera preventive," boxes of pills for curing every disease to which human nature is liable; and India-rubber life preservers.

The presses were turning out *Guide Books to the Gold Fields* as fast as they could be written. They were full of advice on how to go, when to go, what to do when you got there, and how to survive and become rich. One such title was *California and the Way to Get There: With the Official Documents Relating to the Gold Region*, by J. Ely Sherwood (New York, 1848). Another was

The Pocket-Guide to California: A Sea and Land Route Book, Containing A Full Description of the El Dorado. Its Agricultural Resources, Commercial Advantages and Mineral Wealth: Including A Chapter on Gold Formation.

A guidebook was considered indispensable; each pilgrim carried his favorite, complete with maps of the gold fields. For, although everyone knew that gold was lying about all over the place, no one wanted to take any chances of missing it.

Thus the eager gold-miner-to-be had his purse considerably lightened even before he started on his way. He commenced overladen with all kinds of worthless junk, equipment, and merchandise, much of which he discarded long before California hove into sight.

But who cared about prices or costs? "I'm off to California with my washbowl on my knee!"

AROUND CAPE HORN OR BY WAY OF PANAMA TO THE GOLD FIELDS

When a ship was ready to leave, relatives and friends crowded the pier to see the forty-niners off. Often a church service was held, and God's help was asked to protect and guide the young men during their long ocean journey and in the gold fields. Then, amid cheers and tears, salutes from cannon, and the shanties of the sailors, the ship slowly nosed out of the dock and headed out to sea, beginning her long voyage.

Many of the forty-niners kept diaries and have left us descriptive cameos of their adventures at sea and on land and in the gold fields. T. T. Johnson, a forty-niner bound for California, paints a vivid picture of the ship's sailing:

The scene of our departure presented a spectacle ludicrous and extraordinary. The decks of our steamer were crowded to suffocation with departing adventurers and their friends—our ribs were in danger of fracture from pressure of the crowds—our shins from contusions against the gold machines, forcing pumps, crowbars, shovels, axes, picks, pocket-pistols and pick-pockets, and our lungs of collapse from returning the excited cheers of the multitude. The wharves and shipping, including three other ocean steamers, were crowded with a dense throng to witness our departure. . . .

As we passed slowly out of the dock, shouts arose of, "Bring me a pocketful of rocks!" "Don't forget the washers round the Horn." "O, don't you cry for me, dear, I'm coming back again," and "Jim, you forgot your life preserver!" answered by, "Well, I'll get one at the bar." Thus we commenced our long voyage.

Most of the emigrants, outlandishly costumed, were as heavily armed as if going off to fight in a terrible war. They were, continues Johnson,

clad in all sorts of costumes, from a Broadway top-coat and cloth cap, to a boatman's pea jacket and nor-wester, and from a western hunting shirt and wild cat, to a bonafide Mexican blanket and sombrero. Pistols, bowie-knives, rifles and revolvers, slung over our shoulders or stuck in our belts; and one valiant company of fierce and daring men shouldered the terrible musket and flashing bayonet, while around the neck of a distinguished warrior hung the alarum trumpet, to sound the brazen charge to victory or death.

The first few days were often the worst part of the trip for the inexperienced landlubbers. The forty-niners had paid handsomely for their passage, and had received assurances when they bought their tickets that they would have private or semiprivate accommodations. The reality at sea was quite the opposite. Frequently the owners and captains resorted to outright fraud. They packed cabins to the limit in order to make as much money as possible.

Cooped up in their narrow quarters, pitching and toss-

A forty-niner armed for the diggings

ing about, with no one to look after them or care for them, the passengers were cold and wet from the constant dampness of the ocean. Seasickness was common. Most thought they were surely going to die, and many wished that they would, so they could end their sufferings. But after a few days they recovered, and things became bearable.

The meals aboard were a cause for much grumbling. They were monotonous, coarse, and sometimes scanty. There was no refrigeration or means of keeping food fresh. Bread became hard, meat wormy, and the flour was infested with weevils. Worst was the lack of fresh water. J. J. Stillman, a medical doctor bound for El Dorado, comments:

For several days our fare has been very poor—salt junk and stewed apples for dinner one day, with panfuls of moldy seabiscuits and simple pork and beans, without even the condiment of pickels, for the next. This morning our breakfast was ham, mush and molasses and vinegar; the mush was raw and without salt and we would not accept it.

The passengers held a protest meeting, reports Stillman:

The next day we met again and adopted a respectable remonstrance stating our grievances—that we had paid for first class cabin passage, that we were to have the same fare as the Captain and family, instead of which we were fed on food that was coarse, badly cooked and no better than that fed to the crew. When the committee presented it, [the captain] stood on the afterdeck and refused to receive it, abused us all roundly and told us that if he had any more trouble with us, he would fire the magazine and blow us all to h-ll together. We don't fear the threat and doubt his ability to accomplish the alternative. Some of us have higher expectations.

At the few stops the ships made to replenish their supplies, mainly South American ports, the passengers looked forward eagerly to going ashore. There they would stuff themselves on fresh milk, water, iced drinks, and fruit. One argonaut, George Payson, tells of walking a mile through fine sand to reach an orange plantation.

The house, which was small and light, like a huge bird-cage of bamboo, stood in the midst of an orange orchard, where the fruit was hanging on the trees in the greatest profusion. The price demanded was 25¢ a hundred; we were to gather the oranges ourselves. It was a pleasant novelty—this picking oranges as though they had been apples—tasting one here and there and throwing it magnanimously away, if it were not quite first-rate. We selected the sweetest trees and stopping only to pick the thickest of the fruit, we had collected by noon more than 5,000 oranges, which we thought as many as our boat would hold.

Even when the boats were less crowded, feeding the large number of people was a problem. Two meals a day, breakfast and dinner, were served aboard ship. Passengers were summoned by the ringing of bells. Taylor, one of the argonauts, was astonished by the voracious appetites of the gold-seekers.

At the first tinkle of the bell, all hands started as if a shot had exploded among them; conversations were broken off in the middle of a word, the deck was in-

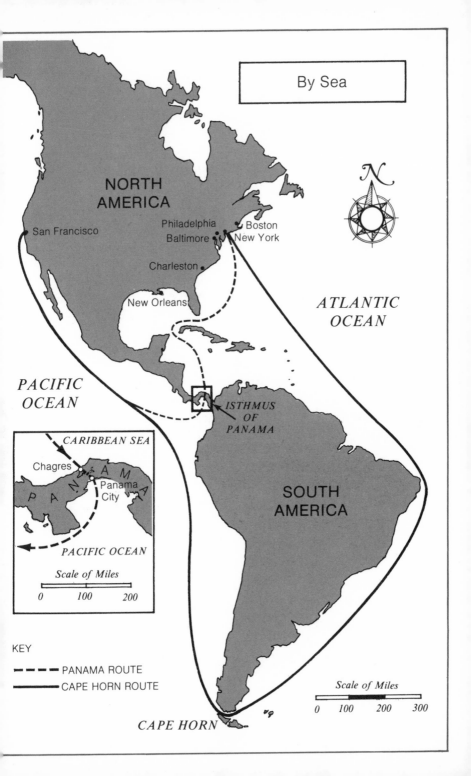

By Sea

NORTH AMERICA

San Francisco

Philadelphia • Boston
Baltimore • New York

Charleston •

New Orleans

ATLANTIC OCEAN

PACIFIC OCEAN

ISTHMUS OF PANAMA

SOUTH AMERICA

CARIBBEAN SEA

Chagres

PANAMA

Panama City

PACIFIC OCEAN

Scale of Miles
0   100   200

CAPE HORN

KEY
- - - PANAMA ROUTE
——— CAPE HORN ROUTE

Scale of Miles
0   100   200   300

stantly cleared, and the passengers stumbling pell-mell down the cabin-stairs, found every seat taken by others, who had probably been sitting in them for half an hour.

There was a confused grabbing motion for a few seconds, and lo! the plates were cleared. A chicken parted in twain as if by magic, each half leaping into an opposite plate, a dish of sweet potatoes vanished before a single hand; beefsteak flew in all directions; and while about half the passengers had their breakfast at once upon their plates, the other half were regaled by a "plentiful lack."

Another hardship the passengers endured was the terrible storms. To many it seemed certain that their ship was about to capsize and sink. On May 9, 1849, Dr. Stillman confided to his diary:

I have not been able to continue the narrative of our voyage owing to the stress of weather. We were in all the horrors of a storm as violent as the one we had so lately passed through. Hail and snow continued during the day, and night brought no relief; no one dared to venture on deck and our situation was an unenviable one. Our attempts to sleep would have been amusing to a disinterested spectator. All the rooms on the lee side were drenched with water from leaks in the deck. Doctors Edwards, Hall and Jones came to my room on the weather side. One sat against the door with his feet against the berth, another against the berth with his feet against the door. Sherwood was in his berth lashed fast, while Dr. Hall was wedged into my berth with me, and we were braced in opposite directions and so managed to keep our place. Thus we passed the night. Sometimes the ship would continue so long on her side that we would fear that the next wave would finish her. We would stare into each other's faces like owls, and then as she righted would collapse again into drowsy indifference.

But worse was yet to come when the ship tried to beat around Cape Horn. The captain and crew attempted to prepare the ship for her ordeal by overhauling her sails and strengthening her riggings. Passage around the Horn could take from a week to a month, depending upon the ferocity of the winds and storms. For the passengers it was a nightmare, an endless ordeal. Constantly wet from the seas breaking over the decks and water running down into their cabins, they tried unsuccessfully to dry themselves out and preserve some semblance of comfort.

Yet, despite seasickness, crowding, poor food, storms, and near sinkings, the forty-niners were sustained through all their adversities by their vision of gold. George Payson put their determination into words:

But I had still no relenting of purpose; through storms and thirst, and burning fever, I was sustained by dreams of golden joy. . . . My calculations, so I thought, were by no means extravagant: $2,000 certain—$20,000 probable —$100,000 possible. I now saw these numbers printed in glaring ciphers and with all the lifelike, seductive reality of a lottery placard, all over the walls of my stateroom. Who would not, for such reward, endure the discomforts of a four months' voyage, although every week should be like the first!

The boredom and tedium of the voyage and their enforced inactivity led the forty-niners to seek numerous ways of amusing themselves and passing the time. Many

Fair weather on the trip around the Horn

kept a diary or journal of their voyage. Others wrote letters to their families and friends, which they would mail upon their arrival in San Francisco. They sorted, arranged, and repacked their equipment. Books and newspapers on board were passed around and read until they were in tatters. Some companies got out a daily or weekly newspaper. On Sunday, religious services were usually held.

The passengers played backgammon, whist, solitaire, chess, and checkers. Card games flourished, and Donaldson tells of an amusing incident:

On the steamship California, the crowd of passengers were so dense that a party of four young men, finding no room for a table on which to play a social game of cards, and seeing a stout man on the cabin floor asleep on the flat of his back, used his stomach for a card-table. It worked well until one of them, becoming excited, threw a trump down on it with such emphasis as to awaken the owner of the stomach. He said: "It's all right with me, boys, go ahead, but use me gently." It was a Baptist minister from near their home.

Although gambling was forbidden by the constitutions of most companies, betting was heavy. Hubert Bancroft, the historian, himself on the way to the gold fields from New York City, remembers how wagers were made on any occasion:

Bets were made on daily distances, on the time of arrival at any point, on the height or weight of any person or thing, on the time in which coat and boots could be taken off and put on, and on anything that happened to strike the fancy, however absurd.

For the first time in their lives, many of the young men had a long period of time on their hands, and they developed new hobbies and skills. Spanish, medicine, astrology, and navigation were studied; amateur theatricals were produced; wood carving and whittling were popular; poetry and prose were written.

In nice weather people basked and lolled around the deck in the shade of the sails, telling stories and playing practical jokes. There were continuous discussions of politics, science, religion, and home, and endless talk and speculation about California and the gold fields. They engaged in wrestling, boxing, vaulting, and handsprings. Payson recounts how they kept themselves occupied:

Soon after we began, one by one, to drop down from our berths; and having drawn on our pantaloons, we shuffled along, towel and washbowl in hand, to the waist of the ship where we were used to perform our ablutions. A fireman's bucket attached to a stout rope had been considerately provided for the use of one hundred passengers.

This important duty being at length accomplished, we proceeded in fine weather to promenade the deck till breakfast. The forenoon was occupied in a great variety of ways. Some disinterested and inquiring individuals kept a constant lookout for sails, sharks and whales, in order to gratify the universal craving for novelty and excitement. Those were the newsmongers and express agents of our little community. A shark could not show his dorsal fin within a cable's length of the ship,—a whale could not wag his tail or blow his nose within five miles,—and a sail could not steal into the wide horizon of the masthead without being at once detected by half a dozen curious eyes, and straightway reported to all below. Various groups on deck were occupied in reading, talking and smoking, or in games of chance or skill. A few bolder spirits have even the hardihood to attempt "Spanish without a master."

But of all their pastimes, music and singing were the favorites. Almost every ship had someone with a fiddle or other instrument. Dancing was also popular, and T. T. Johnson tells of musical evenings aboard ship:

We spent the lovely moonlight evenings with songs and chorus, or in listening to the flute and violin. When our national airs were played, enthusiastic cheers resounded through the ship; the Marseilles hymn elicited three cheers for the French republic; and when finally our gentlemanly and jolly captain performed a sailor hornpipe in first rate style, nine cheers roared around the decks and up the shrouds, till the ship almost danced in chorus.

Stephen Foster's tune "Oh, Susannah" was used by the forty-niners for a parody called "Oh, California." It was extremely popular and is widely reported to have been sung both at sea and on land by forty-niners traveling to California. There are many versions, but all are to the same tune and very similar in content.

I come from Salem City with my washbowl on my knee,
I'm going to California the gold dust for to see.
It rained all night the day I left, the weather it was dry,
The sun so hot I froze to death, oh brother, don't you cry.

CHORUS:
Oh, California, that's the land for me,
I'm bound for San Francisco with my washbowl on my knee.

I jumped aboard the largest ship and traveled on the sea,
And everytime I thought of home, I wished it wasn't me!
The vessel reared like any horse that had of oats a wealth,
I found it wouldn't throw me, so I thought I'd throw myself!

CHORUS

I thought of all the pleasant times we've had together here,
And I thought I ought to cry a bit, but I could not find a tear.
The pilot's bread was in my mouth, the gold dust in my eye,
And though I'm going far away, dear brother, don't you cry.

CHORUS

I soon shall be in Frisco and there I'll look around,
And when I see the golden lumps there, I'll pick them off the ground.
I'll scrape the mountains clean, my boys, I'll drain the rivers dry,
A pocketful of rocks bring home, so brothers, don't you cry.

CHORUS

Not all the argonauts sailed the 15,000 miles around the Horn. Many men traveled the isthmus route, which was shorter and faster. In 1848 the age of the steamship had arrived, and there were five steamships for the Atlantic run between New York and the isthmus and three for the Pacific run. Since so few steamships were available, men would form lines for days and nights in front of the ticket booths. They fought to get aboard any ship that would take them to Chagres, on the east coast of Panama. Steamboat passage was terribly expensive, so all kinds of vessels were hired to make the voyage.

Landing at Chagres, the forty-niners had to find transportation for themselves and their baggage across the isthmus to Panama City. On paper the distance did not seem great—about 60 or 70 miles—but it was a rough, hard trip. There were only the most primitive accommodations along the way, and very few villages or towns. The men had to carry their own blankets and food.

Already impatient to get to the gold fields, the anxiety of the gold-seekers was increased upon meeting successful miners returning from California who had already struck it rich and made their pile. Bayard Taylor, an aspiring prospector, recalls one such incident, shortly after his ship had reached Chagres:

A returning Californian had just reached the place, with a box containing $22,000 in gold dust and a four pound lump in one hand. The impatience and excitement of the passengers, already at high pitch, was greatly increased by his appearance. Life and death were small matters compared with immediate departure from Chagres. Men ran up and down the beach, shouting, gesticulating, and getting feverishly impatient at the deliberate habits of the natives as if their arrival in California would thereby be at all hastened. The boatmen, knowing full well that two more steamers were due the next day, remained provokingly cool and unconcerned. They had not seen six months of emigration without learning something of the American habit of going at full speed.

Living in a different culture, where time and speed were of little importance, the Panamanian boatmen found it hard to understand the anxiety and impatience of the Americans to get going, that a minute lost might mean their failure to reach California in time. The Americans, on their part, regarded the natives as lazy and ignorant, as savages to be bullied into renting their canoes and themselves whether they wanted to do so or not. When the natives raised their charges or did not want to pole the argonauts up the Chagres, the cry went up: "Whip the rascal, fire his den, burn the settlement, annex the isthmus!"

The first part of the trip was up the Chagres River. While the passengers relaxed and contemplated the scenery, it was hard work for the boatmen. They needed all their strength and skill to pole the boat upriver against the current. Bancroft describes the exertions of "two, four or six black, thicklimbed, muscular negroes who propelled the boat up the stream by means of poles at an average speed of a mile an hour."

Bancroft tells how the boatmen took their stand

upon the broadened edges of the canoe, on either side, one end of their pole upon the bottom of the river, and the other placed against their shoulder, smoking with perspiration, their deep chests sending forth volumes of vapor into the vapory air, their swollen sinews strained to their utmost tension, and keeping time in a sort of grunting song, they step steadily along from stem to stern, thus sending the boat rapidly over the water, except when the current is strong.

Upon reaching Gorgona or Cruces, two villages at the end of the river, the gold-seekers disembarked and started bargaining with the natives who would guide them to Panama City. Whether they went by mule or on foot, the journey was one that would not soon be forgotten. It was a narrow, ancient trail winding over the mountains along steep precipices and through streams and jungles. It was the old gold-train road over which the Spanish years before had shipped their treasures from Peru to Spain.

Frank Marryat was a seaman, actor, adventurer, artist,

and British-bred sportsman. He had sailed across the Atlantic Ocean to board a ship at New York City, headed for Panama and thence to the gold fields. He tells of the slow, tortuous progress by muleback over the trail:

With our mules in a string, we plunged at once into a narrow, rocky path in the forest, where palm-trees and creepers shut the light out overhead—splashing through gurgling, muddy streams, that concealed loose and treacherous stones—stumbling over fallen trees that lay across our road—burying ourselves to the mules' girths in filthy swamps, where on either side dead and putrid mules were lying—amidst lightning, thunder and incessant rain, we went at a foot-pace on the road to Panama. The thunderstorm changed the twilight of our covered path to darkness, and one of my mules, missing his footing on the red, greasy clay, falls down under his heavy load. When he gets up, he has to be unpacked, amidst the curses of the muleteer, and packed again, and thus losing half an hour in the pelting storm, we find ourselves the last upon the road.

The journey across the isthmus took about five days. The travelers were eaten alive by mosquitoes, gnats, and other insects; alternately broiled by the sun and soaked by tropical downpours. At overnight stops along the route, they found only the most primitive quarters. Taylor relates how he rented a hammock in one of the native huts which consisted of

a single room, in which all of the household operations were carried on. A notched pole, serving as a ladder, led to a sleeping loft, under the pyramidal roof of thatch. Here a number of the emigrants who arrived late were

Crossing the Isthmus of Panama, 1849 cartoon

stowed away on a rattling floor of cane, covered with hides. After a supper of pork and coffee, I made my day's notes by the light of a miserable starveling candle stuck in an empty bottle, but had not written far before my paper was covered with fleas. The owner of the hut swung my hammock meanwhile, and I turned in to secure it for the night. To lie there was one thing, to sleep another. A dozen natives crowded round the table, drinking their aguardiente and disputing vehemently; the cooking fire was on one side of me, and every one who passed to and fro was sure to give me a thump, while my weight swung the hammock so low, that all the dogs on the premises were constantly rubbing their backs under me.

Worn and weary, the travelers finally reached Panama City to find conditions even worse. There were many more ships on the Atlantic run than on the Pacific one. The forty-niners piled up in Panama City waiting for a boat to take them to San Francisco. The few hotels were filled, and it was impossible to get a room in one for any amount of money. Thus most forty-niners had to live outside the town, in primitive camps. The crowding, lack of sanitation, improper diet, exposure to extreme climate, and weakened condition of many of the argonauts caused widespread disease. There were few doctors, and little medicine or health care was available. Thousands became sick of dysentery, malaria, cholera, and Panama fever. Victims were usually left to take care of themselves; Panama City became a pesthole of misery, sickness, and death.

Some of the would-be miners, after months of waiting,

gave up and went back to the States. They were joined by a steady stream of disillusioned miners who had been to California and were returning home sadder, wiser, and mostly poorer. But most of the emigrants waited for ships to take them on to San Francisco; as their passage money dwindled away they were left penniless. Bancroft jotted down his observations:

Here waiting and watching, some of them for weeks and months for an opportunity to get away, they continued the process of moral declination and decivilization. Fledglings, fresh from their mothers, little lemon-dried men and tall, hairy fellows (armed to the teeth and steaming with perspiration) strolled about the streets, watching the fruit vendors and water-carriers, ogling the bare-breasted girls, pricing hats, looking wistfully at the tempting catalogue of iced drinks through the open doors of the saloons; or entering the churches they would stalk about the isles.

Some few of the aspiring sort studied Spanish or essayed some knowledge of the history of crumbling relics; some played billiards or gambled or got drunk; some fished, gathered shells, braved the sharks and bathed, hunted monkeys and parroquets, or sat under old vine-clad walls gazing at the humming birds as they buzzed about the flowers. Some died of fever; others killed themselves by drinking villainous liquors, eating excessively of fruit, or by overdoing with pills, patent medicines, cholera preventives and like supposed antidotes to supposed internal diseases. Once seized with sickness and without a faithful comrade, a man's chance for recovery was small, for already a coating of callous indifference to the sufferings of others seemed to be enclosing the hearts of many

Waiting at Panama for the steamer, magazine cartoon, 1849

of these adventurers, and a pale, fever-stricken stranger was too often shunned like a leper.

When the steamship *California*, already filled with gold-seekers from Peru, docked at Panama City, it found 1,500 forty-niners waiting. The *California* had room for only 100 more passengers. Men were desperate to leave Panama City, and almost any price was paid for a ticket, even as much as $600. The *California* squeezed in 500 more passengers and steamed off for San Francisco. Left behind were 1,000 howling, disappointed forty-niners. Frantic, some of them hired dugouts and fishing craft to make the long trip up to San Francisco. Most of these returned within a month or were never heard from again.

Feelings toward the presence of the Peruvians on board the *California* ran high, and were assuaged only when a circular issued by General Persefir F. Smith, who was on his way to California to take over military command of the United States forces there, was read aloud to the disappointed argonauts left behind in Panama. General Smith made it clear that, in his opinion, California gold was to be only for true-blooded Americans.

The laws of the United States inflict the penalty of fine and imprisonment on trespassers in the public lands. As nothing can be more unreasonable or unjust, than the conduct pursued by persons not citizens of the United States, who are flocking from all parts to search for and carry off gold belonging to the United States in California; and as such conduct is in direct violation of law, it will therefore become my duty, immediately on my arrival there, to put these laws in force, to prevent their infraction in future, by punishing with the penalties prescribed by law, those who offend....

An ominous portent this, for the future of Orientals, Indians, Blacks, and other undesirable "foreigners" in the gold fields!

The crowding on the Pacific steamships was unbelievable. Describing these conditions, Bancroft wrote:

The steerage passengers were treated more like beasts than human beings; to the shipowners they were but so much freight to be carried at so much a head. Their sufferings and whether they lived or died, were matters of their own. They were bedded like swine and fed like swine. Instead of a trough, a broad board shelf was suspended from the ceiling, which served as a table, greasy and clothless, furnished with tin cups and plates and pewter spoons, and on which were placed huge pans or kettles of food, stews, beans and the like. Droves, one after another, were let in through a gate, and after they had fed a while, they were driven off by their sooty overseers.

Besides the three steamboats, sailing ships, whalers, or anything at all that floated sailed to Panama and loaded up for the trip to San Francisco. Frequently tickets were disposed of through a lottery in order to prevent rioting.

Many of the forty-niners carried yellow fever and cholera with them onto the crowded ships, and epidemics often broke out aboard. Wrote Marryat:

I had secured a dog-hole of a cabin, and was no sooner on board than my wife, worn out by fatigue and anxiety, was attacked by violent fever. There were two young doctors on board, but both were attacked shortly after we started. Then the epidemic (an aggravated, intermittent fever) broke out among the passengers, who—crowded in the hold as thick as blacks in a slaver—gave way to *fear and could not be moved from the lower deck, and so lay weltering in their filth.*

During this time, I could get no medicine or attention and my wife was in the last stage of prostration.

The epidemic raged and from the scuttle-hole of our small cabin, we could hear the splash of the bodies as they were tossed overboard with very little ceremony.

Marryat and his wife were lucky, for both recovered. Despite the short trip, mortality on the Pacific steamers was much heavier than on the sailboats going around the Horn. The steamers were more crowded; the forty-niners were weakened by their journey across the isthmus; and disease took a heavier toll. There was also a greater incidence of shipwreck on the steamboats. Steering close to shore in their race to reach San Francisco and lacking accurate charts, they ran aground onto rocks and reefs. There were no lighthouses or buoys to warn them of the dangers. Another peril was fire, a constant threat on a steamer.

Finally the ships did make land. By July of 1849, more than five hundred ships, flying the flags of almost every nation, loaded with gold-seekers from all over the world, had sailed into San Francisco Bay. The harried passengers, anxious over their delay in reaching the gold fields, tumbled over the sides of their vessel into the first small boats they could find that would take them ashore. By nightfall, the crews, too, usually had deserted. Their empty ships lay abandoned.

In 1849, a total of 39,000 argonauts came to San Francisco by sea. But the greatest rush was yet to come by the overland route.

Blood-Red Roses

Our boots and clothes are all in pawn Go down, you
blood - red ros - es, go down! And it's might - y draft - y
round Cape Horn Go down, you blood - red ros - es,
go down! Oh, you pinks and po - sies
Go down, you blood - red ros - es, go down!

SOLO: Our boots and clothes are all in pawn

CHORUS: Go down, you blood-red roses, go down!

SOLO: And it's mighty drafty round Cape Horn

CHORUS: Go down, you blood-red roses, go down!

SOLO: Oh, you pinks and posies

CHORUS: Go down, you blood-red roses, go down!

SOLO: Oh, you pinks and posies

CHORUS: Go down, you blood-red roses, go down!

SOLO: You've had your advance and to sea must go

CHORUS: Go down, you blood-red roses, go down!

SOLO: Chasing whales through the frost and snow

CHORUS: Go down, you blood-red roses, go down!

SOLO: Oh, you pinks and posies

CHORUS: Go down, you blood-red roses, go down!

SOLO: Oh, you pinks and posies

CHORUS: Go down, you blood-red roses, go down!

SOLO: My old mother, she wrote to me

CHORUS: Go down, you blood-red roses, go down!

SOLO: "My dearest son, come home from sea."

CHORUS: Go down, you blood-red roses, go down!

SOLO: Oh, you pinks and posies

CHORUS: Go down, you blood-red roses, go down!

SOLO: Oh, you pinks and posies

CHORUS: Go down, you blood-red roses, go down!

SOLO: But around Cape Horn we all must go

CHORUS: Go down, you blood-red roses, go down!

SOLO: Round Cape Horn through the ice and snow

CHORUS: Go down, you blood-red roses, go down!

SOLO: Oh, you pinks and posies

CHORUS: Go down, you blood-red roses, go down!

SOLO: Oh, you pinks and posies

CHORUS: Go down, you blood-red roses, go down!

OVERLAND BY THE
CALIFORNIA TRAIL

From Missouri and Iowa to Massachusetts and New York, there were thousands of people who could not afford the expensive sea voyage. Others did not live near the sea. The route for them was by land. The favorite starting points for the journey were Independence and St. Joseph, Missouri, and Council Bluffs, Iowa, all on the Missouri River. One emigrant woman recalled:

The Missouri is considered the starting point—from this river is time reckoned and it matters not how far you have come, this is the point to which they all refer, for the question is never, when did you leave home? but, when did you leave the Missouri River?

It was a 2,100-mile trip from these starting points to the gold fields if you traveled along the California Trail. The forty-niners were greenhorns and were unaware of the tremendous undertaking they were facing. Their minds were on gold nuggets. As one emigrant wrote home:

The great majority now crossing the plains were profoundly ignorant of what was before them when starting

—had no idea of what an outfit consisted of, and in short, looked upon crossing the prairies as nothing but a pleasure trip, where killing buffalo, wolf hunting, etc., formed the prominent features.

At Independence, St. Joseph, or Council Bluffs, the travelers joined one of the wagon trains forming on the outskirts of the city. The emigrants spent their waiting time checking over their equipment and supplies, making sure that they had not forgotten anything, poring over their maps and guidebooks. There was constant visiting and talking among members of the different wagons, every man giving his opinion as to what the trip would be like. G. W. Thissell traveled from his home in Morgan County, Ohio, by steamboat to St. Louis and then on to St. Joseph. Commenting on the wild excitement and anticipation, Thissell noted:

At St. Joseph every available camping ground was occupied. Men were rushing to and fro, all eager to buy mules, horses and oxen for the journey. There the emigrants crossed the Missouri River and took the trail for California.

The weather was cold; the throng increased; the excitement ran high. Men impatient, bought feed and extra teams to haul it, crossed the river and left for the gold fields.

One of the organized groups consisted of fourteen wagons. In them were sixty-six young men from Washington, D.C., piloted by their elected captain, Joseph Goldborough Bruff. The men all wore gray uniforms and were armed with rifles, pistols, bowie knives, and hatchets. Bruff, a draftsman who had worked for the Bureau of Topographical Engineers, kept a detailed journal of their experiences crossing the plains. One of the most important jobs was learning how to handle their teams and wagons. As Bruff commented, this was not an easy job: "Next to exposure to bad weather, the mulebreaking job comes hard on the boys. Most of them knew as much about mules when they arrived here, as the mules did about them."

The wagon trains started out in early May, as soon as the grass on the prairies had grown enough to support the teams and cattle. Each train wanted to be first, to be in the lead and be assured of fresh grass and water. They would thus avoid long waits at the ferries and rutted roads.

The first day out, all was excitement and confusion. "On to California" was the cry. Wagons had names and slogans printed on their canvases: *Live Hoosier, Wild Yankee, Rough and Ready, Enterprise, Gold Hunter, Meet You at Sutter's Fort.*

One thing the emigrants were well aware of was that they had a strict time limit for the trip. All knew the fate of the Donner party, which had gotten trapped in the mountains by an early snowfall in October 1846, as they reached Truckee Pass. The forty-niners had four months, five at the most, in which to reach California. The wagons had to average about fourteen to sixteen miles a day. They had to keep on going. There was literally no place to stop, no house between the Missouri River and Salt Lake City, or between the latter and the gold regions.

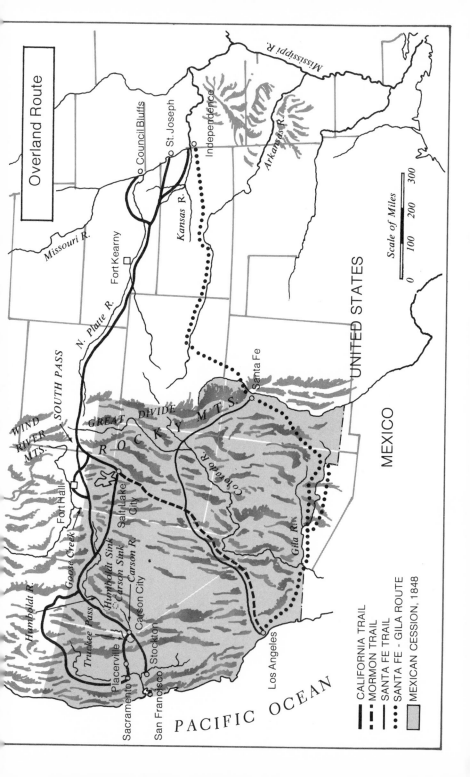

Overland Route

Mississippi R.

o Council Bluffs
o St. Joseph
o Independence

Missouri R.

Kansas R.

Arkansas R.

Fort Kearny

N. Platte R.

SOUTH PASS

WIND
RIVER
MTS.

GREAT   DIVIDE

R O C K Y   M'T S.

Fort Hall

Goose Creek

Humboldt R.

Humboldt Sink
Carson Sink
Carson R.
Carson City

Salt Lake
City

Colorado R.

Santa Fe

Gila R.

MEXICO

UNITED STATES

Truckee Pass

Placerville
Stockton
Sacramento
San Francisco

Los Angeles

PACIFIC OCEAN

Scale of Miles
0   100   200   300

CALIFORNIA TRAIL
MORMON TRAIL
SANTA FE TRAIL
SANTA FE - GILA ROUTE
MEXICAN CESSION, 1848

After a few days of travel, wagon trains stretched clear back to Independence. Bottlenecks quickly developed at most of the ferries and fords on the rivers. Bruff wrote:

In every direction, as far as can be seen, the country is speckled with the white tents and wagons of the emigrants. The crowd at the ferry is a dense mass—fighting for precedence to cross. As soon as a wagon enters the boat, the next moves down to the edge of the bank, and the long mass of wagons in the rear close down. And this goes on from earliest dawn till midnight, day after day.

Although annoying to the emigrants, these delays were in fact desirable. They spaced the migration out and prevented too great a concentration at any one spot along the trail.

By the time the voyagers reached the Kansas River, they had traveled about a hundred miles. Men had learned how to handle a wagon and team. Women had learned to set up camp and make things comfortable. The animals had settled down to their task of pulling the wagons. Bruff quipped: "Our teamsters have quite an ordeal to pass through, to acquire the honorary degree of M.D. (Mule Driver)."

After crossing over the Kansas River there was a period of adjustment and reorganization among most trains. Wagons were constantly being made lighter as "necessary equipment" was abandoned bit by bit. Bruff observed:

A walnut book case found, new, of gothic pattern, broke it up for fuel—fine doors and drawers boiled our coffee. Bottom strewn with clothes, boots, shoes, hats, lead, iron, tin-ware, trunks, meat, wheels, wagon beds, mining tools & c., & c.—& dead oxen. Looked more like

*the trail of a discomfitted army than anything else I
could think of.*

At the start of the journey, the greatest part of a wagon
load consisted of food. Diet was limited to staples that
could be carried along and would not spoil. Flour, crack-
ers, hardtack, cornmeal, rice, beans, salt, sugar, coffee,
and dried fruit were the mainstays. Bacon was popular
but often became rancid. The overlanders supplemented
their food by hunting and fishing and gathering berries,
wild onions, and greens. The diet was monotonous, but
scurvy and other dietary deficiencies seemed unknown.
Bad water and spoiled food caused much dysentery.

After leaving the Kansas, the travelers crossed numerous other rivers and finally neared the valley of the
Platte. For hundreds of miles they would follow this river
westward. Alonzo Delano, an emigrant from Ottawa, Illinois, described his feelings on reaching this stage of his
journey:

*A little before noon we saw the grass-covered sand hills
which bounded the valley of the Platte and we were
some hours in ascending the gentle slope to them. As
we rose to the apex of the last hill, the broad valley of
the Platte lay before us, as level as a floor, and the great
artery of the Missouri, with its turbid, muddy waters, a
mile in width, divided by Grand Island, came in sight.
Here, too, was a scene of active life. Here the road from
old Fort Kearney united with the St. Joseph road, and
for the whole distance in view, up and down the river,
before and behind us, long trains were in motion or en-
camped on the grassy bottom, and we could scarcely
realize that we were in an Indian country, from the scene*

Sketches from Joseph Bruff's Journal, 1849 (Above) Fortyniners
crossing the Missouri (Below) Camp at St. Joseph's Missouri

of civilized life before us, and this was all caused by the magic talisman of gold. What will be the end? Who can foresee our future destiny?

Some people, discouraged, turned back because of sickness or inadequate wagons and teams. Some just lost heart and were scared of the hardships yet to come. They had "seen the elephant" and "eaten its ears." While they still could, the doubters and the quitters gave up and returned to civilization.

The camp began to stir at daybreak. The cattle guards rode in. Women began to build up the fires, and breakfast was quickly made and quickly eaten. The teams were hitched up, the wagons aligned, and the captain of the train gave the signal to start. Whips cracked, drivers shouted, and mules and oxen clumsily started off. Well before midday, the wagons stopped for nooning at a site previously selected by advance scouts. People and animals rested and ate their lunch. It was a long halt, usually two hours or more if it was very hot. The afternoons were more wearing and seemed to last forever. Before sundown, the spot selected for the evening camp came into view. Wagons were pulled into a rough circle, and the oxen were unyoked.

Women prepared supper; children gathered firewood. There was little wood except along the river, and many emigrants made their first acquaintance with buffalo chips, finding them quite satisfactory as fuel. Wrote Thissell:

June 20th: The train reached the sandhills. Not a tree or shrub could be seen. Not a stick of wood could be found. Sand. Sand everywhere and cooking must be done. But the women and children proved themselves equal to the occasion. It was amusing to see them, old and young, gathering buffalo chips for fuel. As none but the driest ones would burn, and as it required at least a bushel of chips to cook a meal, it was no easy task. Some of the chips looked as though they might be fifty years old. They were white as cotton and as light as feathers, and burned like charcoal.

The men looked to their teams and wagons; the captain and the scouts went over the day's journey and outlined plans for the morrow; hunters rode into camp with game they had caught. Supper was ready; it was much the same as breakfast. As the sun went down, the prairies cooled off, and a big fire was built. The people, rested and more at ease now, gathered around it.

Thrown upon their own resources, the forty-niners made their own amusements. Frequently other wagon trains were nearby, and people visited back and forth, exchanging experiences and reminiscing about home. Always there was talk about the latest news from the gold fields. Old newspapers were exchanged and eagerly read.

"The most pleasant part of the trip," recalled Thissell, "was around the camp-fire. Supper over, dishes and pots out of the way, we would gather around the camp-fire and relate the scenes of the day and spin long yarns. Some played the violin, others the accordian. A few would play cards, while the young men would sing their favorite California songs."

As the hour got late, the emigrants made their beds. If it was a clear night, they just camped out. The night guards went out on watch; the fire quickly burned down. Soon all was still and dark.

A popular ballad, sung around many a campfire, told of two forty-niners, Sweet Betsey and her lover, Ike.

Sweet Betsey from Pike

Oh,
don't you re - mem - ber sweet Bet - sey from Pike, Who
crossed the big moun - tains with her lov - er Ike, With
two yoke of ox - en, a large yel - low dog, A —

tall Shang- hai roos - ter and one spot - ted hog.

Chorus

Too - ra - lai oo - ra - lai oo - ra - lai a.

Oh, don't you remember sweet Betsey from Pike,
Who crossed the big mountains with her lover Ike,
With two yoke of oxen, a large yellow dog,
A tall Shanghai rooster and one spotted hog.

Tooralai ooralai ooralai a.

One evening, quite early they camped on the Platte,
'Twas near by the road on a green shady flat,
Where Betsey, sore-footed, lay down to repose—
With wonder Ike gazed on that Pike County rose

CHORUS

Their wagons broke down with a terrible crash,
And out on the prairie rolled all kinds of trash;
A few little baby clothes done up with care—
'Twas rather suspicious, though all on the square.

CHORUS

The Shanghai ran off, and their cattle all died,
That morning the last piece of bacon was fried;
Poor Ike was discouraged and Betsey got mad,
The dog drooped his tail and looked wondrously sad.

CHORUS

They stopped at Salt Lake to inquire the way,
When Brigham declared that sweet Betsey should stay;
But Betsey got frightened and ran like a deer,
When Brigham stood pawing the ground like a steer.

CHORUS

They soon reached the desert, where Betsey gave out,
And down in the sand she lay rolling about;
While Ike, half-distracted, looked on with surprise,
Saying "Betsey get up, you'll get sand in your eyes."

CHORUS

Sweet Betsey got up in a great deal of pain,
Declared she'd go back to Pike County again;
But Ike gave a sigh and they fondly embraced,
And they traveled along with his arm round her waist.

CHORUS

This Pike County couple got married of course,
And Ike became jealous—obtained a divorce;
Sweet Betsey, well satisfied, said with a shout,
"Good-bye, you big lummox, I'm glad you backed out!"

CHORUS

Along with the team, the most important piece of equipment was the wagon. Despite the evidence of Western movies and television programs, the pioneers did not haul big Conestoga wagons, which were much too heavy and cumbersome for the California Trail. Forty-niner vehicles were more like farm wagons, and the emigrants tried to make them as strong yet light-weight as possible. Strength was achieved by a careful selection of the proper kind of wood for each part. Most wagons had neither springs nor brakes. Springs were not too important as the wagons moved slowly, at the rate of about two miles an hour. The problem of braking was solved by locking the wagon wheels with a chain. There were no service stations along the route, and the travelers had to do their own repairs and lubrication. A tar bucket was carried, hanging from the rear axle, and grease was liberally applied on all moving parts.

After several weeks on the trail, the emigrants had become well acquainted with the hardships they had to face. Accidents were common and death frequent. One man was seriously wounded by the chance discharge of his gun. Another was run over trying to stop his runaway team. A third man fell from his wagon, which passed over him and shattered his leg.

Some trains were fortunate enough to have a doctor, but, isolated on the plains, there was little even a doctor could do for the more seriously injured or sick. Graves along the trail were a frequent sight. Some were marked by a stick with the victim's name and date of death; others were just small mounds of earth covered by a few rocks.

Throughout his journal, Bruff made references to these graves, and in June 1849, he noted

4 graves close together, on right of trail, one mile above the Ford, South Fork of the Platte—

C. Taylor, Tenn. David Amick, Mo.
Cholera & typhus Aged 35

Dr. J. T. Boon, Mo. J. Smith, Mo.
Aged 29   Cholera
        Aged 24

Another entry read:

Jno. Hoover, died June 18, 49
Age 12 years. Rest in peace,
Sweet boy, for thy travels are over

Cholera was a constant and frightening threat. It was unbelievable how suddenly it could strike, sweeping a man off his feet and into his grave. There was a violent cholera outburst in June 1849. Bruff mentions a one-week period in which he passed the graves of eight victims of this disease. Thissell gives this description:

The cholera appeared in the train and almost every day we buried a man.

I shall never forget the scene and the experience of last night. Not a man closed his eyes in sleep. During the night Hi Dudley, Jack Snider and Ben Ferguson died. The sick and dying are in every tent. No doctor to be had and but little can be done. We had no cholera remedies except Ayer's Pain Killer, and that gave no relief. Many were sick only a few hours, and then died. No hope of relief until we reach the mountains, where we will have cool nights and pure, cold water.

Weather changed quickly on the plains, and fearful storms, such as the emigrants had never experienced, overtook them and almost drowned them out. An Englishman, William Kelly, Jr., had come to America to join the overland gold rush. His description of a rainstorm on the prairie portrays the cold and wetness of the emigrants:

We then commenced our splashing march through the water, not making more than a mile an hour; nor had we proceeded at this snail's pace over a few miles, when our leading wagon got stuck fast and deep in a slough. The mules being so jaded and cowed they could not be got to pull an ounce; while every moment's pause caused the whole train to settle down so in the soft earth, that it almost looked as if we were destined to remain fixed in the mud until the waters subsided.

The rain now changed into sleet that completely benumbed us, depriving the drivers of all feelings in their fingers to hold the reins. We did not make over nine miles and had not even the consolation of hitting on a dry camping ground; so that the men became woefully depressed, some of them looking as if labouring under the premonitory symptoms of ague. Those not on guard huddled themselves into the wagons to try and generate animal heat by close contact.

The crossing of rivers in flood was hazardous for the pioneers. Mules and wagons could be swept away by the swift currents, and many a man lost his life trying to save them. The prairie, too, had its dangers. It was so flat, such an endless sea of swaying grass, that people often got lost if they strayed too far from their wagon train. One company waited for the return of a man and boy, lost while hunting stray cattle, for three days.

Plagued by gnats and insects, suffering from the constant dust which choked and blinded them, the argonauts kept on going. Kelly described a siege of sand ticks:

We came to the camp ground and we were not much troubled with mosquitoes, but there was a sand-tick, like a small clock, that crawled all over us, finally fixing on delicate places, where they stuck themselves into the skin with a tenacity that tested the strength of the fingernails in disclosing them. Our skins looked as if we spent the night under soot drops; but the worst of it was they got established in legions in the buffalo robes, from which there was no combing of them.

Some held on to their sense of humor and their optimism.

The mosquitoes here have been lied about. None are as large as turkeys; the biggest one I saw was no bigger than a crow.

The settlers established their own "telegraph line" to let those coming behind them know what had happened up to this point. They nailed sheets of paper to the trunks of trees; these contained the date, the names of the travelers, where they came from, and incidents along the way. When they reached the buffalo region, they would write their message on a bleached buffalo skull or shoulder blade.

Grafitti was very common even during these times. In his journal entry of July 9, Bruff commented:

All the accessible faces of blocks and cliffs, were marked and inscribed with names, initials and dates. This peculiar vanity has been displayed all along the route, from our frontier down into the valley of the Sacramento. Nothing escapes that can be marked upon—buffalo skulls, stumps, logs, trees, rocks, etc., even the slabs at the heads of graves are all marked by this propensity of "penciling by the way." The singular feature is that of marking initials; for instance A.S.S., as if everyone should know who he was.

Surprisingly enough, although there was no established law, there was relatively little crime on the trail. The emigrants were mainly law-abiding people with an ingrained respect for order and fair play. In the main, good fellowship, charity, and hospitality prevailed. When a crime was committed, the men of the train held an informal trial, rendered a verdict, and speedily carried out the sentence.

Fort Kearney on the Platte River in Nebraska was the first real stopping place along the trail. Here many of the emigrants rested awhile and repaired their wagons. By now buffalo were a common sight, and few argonauts could withstand the temptation of hunting the buffalo. "This has been an exciting day for our company," noted Kelly:

About sunrise on looking to the [river] bottoms, which are here three or four miles wide, to our astonished eye, we beheld it literally black with buffalo. In an instant all was bustle and excitement. Every man unconnected with the teams seized his rifle and spurred on to meet them at the point where they would cross the road. And I presume that not less than fifty buffalo were slaughtered that morning, whereas not three in all were used. Such a wanton destruction of buffalo, the main dependence of the Indians for food, is certainly reprehensible.

Although often angered by the thoughtless slaughter of their game, the Indians generally practiced restraint toward the whites. There were isolated instances of Indians attacking strays from the wagon trains or stealing horses and oxen, but the Indians were much too intelligent to attack the heavily armed wagon trains. Sometimes the Indians rode into the camps to trade and bargain for food, arms, and ammunition.

Finally the emigrants came to South Pass in the Rockies, which marked the Great Divide. Many of the forty-niners were under the impression that they were almost there, but California was still a long way off. As they descended through South Pass, they could see the ragged and bleak ranges of the Wind River Mountains on their right and the white-covered peaks of the Colorado Rockies to the south and southwest.

The emigrants now picked their way across deserts, which alternated with swift rivers and rough mountain country. Nine or ten days later, they reached Fort Hall, a trading post of the Hudson Bay Company. They had traveled about 1,200 miles from Independence but were still only little more than halfway to their destination.

By now the journey seemed endless; all sense of time had been lost. The farther they went, the rougher became the trail. From Goose Creek to the Humboldt River was a difficult trip of about ninety-five miles. According to all the diaries and letters, it was here that the effects of the long trip began to tell. Already worn down by their hardships, both animals and humans weakened more rapidly; and many just fell apart. It was not so much new difficulties; it was more a case of facing up to hardship on top of all the other troubles they had endured. They had been on the trail for around three months, and now they must face nature at its worst. There was no recourse but to go forward, for if you could not get through from here, neither could you turn back.

The vicious heat of the desert seemed to drain the energy and life out of animals and people. Describing the feelings of his fellow emigrants, Thissell commented:

Our train is in a state of rebellion. Two men quarreled last night. John Pritchard stabbed William Smith with a dirk and killed him. Pritchard had a trial and was acquitted. Every one is cross and ill-natured. The cattle are restless and will not feed. Two men are sick. Some want to travel with the men, die or not die. The whole train is on the war-path. Everything is wrong. The food is poor. Wood is scarce. Wind is blowing a gale from the north, cold as a Christmas morning in Dakota.

Reader, did you ever eat a meal in an old California corral, with the wind blowing thirty miles an hour, holding your hat on with one hand, trying to appease nature with the other, your bread and meat covered with dust and dirt, the gravel and sand flying so thick you could not see? If not, you know but little of the many trials the emigrants of '49–'50 had.

The emigrants followed the Humboldt for the next 365 miles, to the Humboldt Sink. The wagons plodded along day after day. The sun blazed down, the powdered dust covered everything. Many of the trains took to resting during the day and moving at night. Reuben Cole Shaw, an argonaut from South Boston, who had left his wife and infant son to cross the plains and make his fortune, wrote bitterly about the Humboldt:

There is not a fish nor any other living thing to be found in its waters and there is not timber enough in 300 miles of its desolate valley to make a snuff-box, or sufficient vegetation along its banks to shade a rabbit,

Sketches from Joseph Bruff's Journal, 1849   (Above) A Waterhole
on the plains   (Below) Military encampment near Fort Hall

Commencement of a bastioned stockade.

while its waters contain the alkali to make soap for a nation, and after winding its sluggish way through a desert within a desert, it sinks, disappears and leaves inquisitive men to ask how, why, when and where?

Many of the pools were filled with alkali, and the emigrants had to be constantly on their guard to make sure their half-crazed animals did not drink these waters. Slowly, defiantly, desperately, the wagons continued onward. At the Sink they rested, cut grass, and took the last water they would find before crossing the Forty Mile Desert. This was one of the most dreaded *journadas*, or desert crossings. It had no water, was wholly without vegetation, and was thick with alkali dust. The emigrants traveled two days and a night with no stopping except to rest the teams briefly now and then. Describing the sufferings of the emigrants, Shaw wrote:

On the last twenty miles of our journey we passed the skeletons of many animals which had perished before they could reach the water. Oxen died with their yokes still on them, while horses and mules lay dead in their harness and property of all kinds, even bedding was scattered along the road. Wagons, from which the canvas tops had not been removed, were shrinking in the hot sun, with their tires ready to fall from their wheels. Oxen, after making a desperate fight for their lives, perished within a mile of the river. . . . While everything along this road gave evidence of their having been terrible suffering by both man and beast.

What a gorgeous sight the Carson River was to the eyes of the emigrants! A long, hard pull still lay ahead, and they had to cross the Sierra Nevadas, but absolutely nothing could be as bad as the desert. The pioneers had passed the supreme test of the trail; from here on, you could make it by wagon, pack mule, or on foot. The lure of gold was strong now, and new hope seemed to rise within them. Writing on August 10, "Along the Humboldt," Thissell described their anticipation:

Today we met six Mormons returning from California. The report they gave us of the gold mines and the gold dust they showed us, set every man wild to push on and reach the mines.

This was the first gold dust many of us had seen. Some of it coarse, lumps as large as a man's thumb.

We forgot the hardships we had endured and the difficulties yet to overcome before we reach the mines.

Emotionally and physically worn out by their long trip, and used to the proud mounted warriors of the Plains, the emigrants did not react positively to the new type of Indian they met in Nevada and California. On foot, without horse, wearing few clothes, living in rude dirt and bark dwellings, the California Indians must have made a poor showing in the eyes of the forty-niners.

To these Indians, the passage of the emigrant trains through their lands had often spelled disaster. Their few waterholes had been fouled with dead and decaying oxen and mules, the sparse growth of plants and grass had been consumed, and the small game had been driven away. The Indians felt that the white man should pay for this loss, by allowing the Indians a mule or an ox for food. The whites had so much compared with what the Indians had, surely it could easily be shared. But the forty-niners regarded this as stealing and objected strenuously. They accused the Indians of taking anything that was not nailed down. The attitude of most whites toward these Indians is reflected in Kelly's journal:

We are now entering the confines of the Digger Indian territory, the most degraded and debased of all the Indian race, the refuse and dregs of savage society.

They exist, as their name denotes, on roots dug from the earth, vermin and crickets, although with ordinary exertion, they could kill sufficient deer, antelope, and mountain sheep for sustenation, the skins of which would afford them a partial covering.

Their territory covers a great, but for the most part, barren expanse, extending over the Sierra Nevada, into the northern extremity of Alta California. They are a terrible pest and nuisance to travellers and emigrants, for, they are content to fire their arrows at night amongst the animals, hoping to wound or cripple some, so that they will have to be left behind, when they become their prey.

Humboldt River and the head of the Sacramento are the places where they are the most numerous; but they are fast dwindling in numbers, for trappers and travellers shoot them down without hesitation or remorse wherever they meet them.

An estimated 20,000 people started along the California Trail in 1849, and of these about 750 died along the way. Many arrived in California sick and wasted, never to recover from the effects of the trip. Half the wagons and half the animals never made it.

The stragglers numbered in the thousands. Many of these would have perished, but the Californians, despite their preoccupation with gold, organized relief parties and sent out men with extra mules and rations. These rescuers advanced eastward along the three trails leading into California and helped the distressed travelers.

The Fools of Forty-Nine

1. When gold was found in for-ty-eight, the peo-ple said 'twas gas, And some were fools e-nough to think the lumps were made of brass, But

they soon were sat - is - fied and start - ed off __ to mine, They bought a ship came round the Horn in the fall of for - ty nine. Then they thought of

C IV

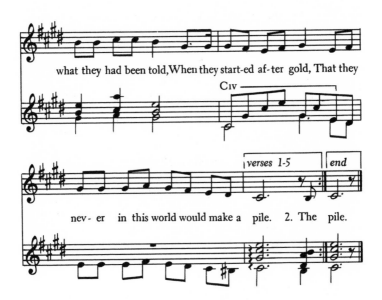

what they had been told, When they start-ed af-ter gold, That they

C IV —

| verses 1-5 | end

nev - er in this world would make a pile. 2. The pile.

When gold was found in forty-eight, the people said 'twas gas,
And some were fools enough to think the lumps were made of
brass,
But they soon were satisfied and started off to mine,
They bought a ship came round the Horn in the fall of forty-
nine.

CHORUS:
Then they thought of what they had been told,
When they started after gold,
That they never in this world would make a pile.

The poor, the old, the rotten scows were advertised to sail,
From New Orleans with passengers, but they must pump and bail,
The ships were crowded more than full, but some hung on behind,
And others dived off from the wharf and swam till they were blind.

CHORUS

With rusty pork and stinking beef and rotten wormy bread
With captains too that never were as high as the mainmast head,
The steerage passengers would rave and swear they'd paid their passage
They wanted something more to eat besides Bologna sausage.

CHORUS

And they begun to cross the plains with oxen, holler and 'haw';
And steamers they began to run as far as Panama,
And there for months the people stayed that started after gold,
And some returned disgusted with the lies they had been told.

CHORUS

The people died on every route, they sickened and died like sheep,
And those at sea before they were dead were launched into the deep,
And those that died crossing the Plains fared not as well as that,
For a hole was dug and they was dumped along the terrible Platte.

CHORUS

CALIFORNIA BEFORE THE
GOLD RUSH

The country the gold-seekers came to was a land of magnificent proportions, of great natural diversity, of extremes and opposites. Nature had done nothing on a small scale. California itself was huge. All of New England, New York, and Pennsylvania could have fitted within her borders. Her coastline of 1,264 miles almost equaled the distance between Boston and Charleston, South Carolina. There were two major mountain chains —the Coastal Range, which extends along the Pacific Coast; and the inland Sierra Nevadas—both of which run north and south through most of California's length.

Lying between the two mountain ranges and separating them was the great Central Valley, approximately 450 miles long and 50 miles wide. This valley was fed by two main rivers: in the north, the Sacramento which flows southward; and in the central area, the San Joaquin, which flows in a northerly direction. Meeting about a hundred miles east of San Francisco, the two rivers joined together and flowed westward toward the sea, before they emptied into magnificent San Francisco Bay. The two rivers were fed by numerous tributaries stream-

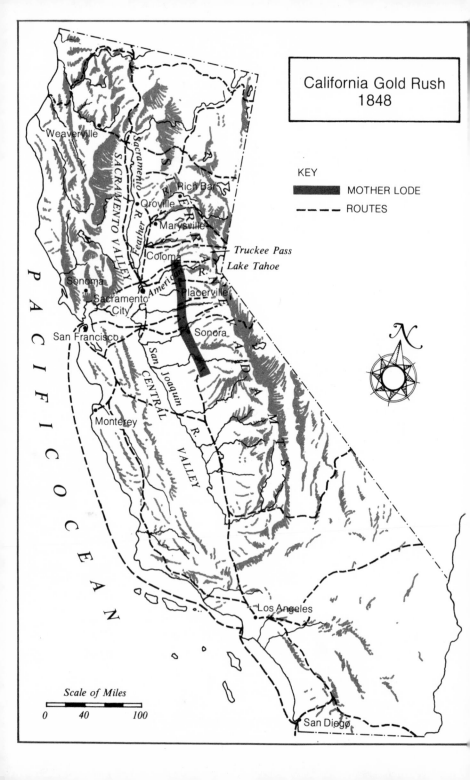

California Gold Rush
1848

KEY

MOTHER LODE

ROUTES

ing down the foothills of the Sierra Nevadas. Buried in the foothills and the torrents of the Sierras was the gold that was to make California's name known throughout the world.

California's climate was gentle, unique. She enjoyed a dry mild temperature with little humidity. Her magnificent redwood and sequoia forests, the largest and oldest living things in the world, covered the coastal and central regions north of the Great Valley. The slopes of the Sierras were thick with virgin pines of all varieties, and in the spring and summer they were alive with brilliant and beautiful wildflowers.

California's hills and plains were filled with game, herds of elk, black-tailed deer, and antelope. Coyotes, grizzly bears, badgers, rabbits, and fox were abundant. The skies were heavy with flocks of wild geese and other waterfowl. The mountain streams were rich with salmon and trout.

Within California's boundaries dwelt over 200,000 Indians. This was a large number, considering that only about a million Indians lived on the mainland of the United States at that time. These were people of the Stone Age. They owned no beasts of burden, were not warlike, practiced little formal government, kept no written records, and did not know the use of metals. The Indians maintained their culture and way of life in peace and harmony with nature and, usually, with one another. They believed and put into practice the theory that all animals and plants were their brothers and that all things were dependent upon one another. All were members of the same world; all were a part of nature.

Geographically cut off from the rest of the world by

Kent Middle School
Media Center

the Pacific Ocean, the Coastal and Sierra ranges, and the Rocky Mountains, as well as by deserts and canyons, the California Indians lived in isolation from other cultures. Each tribe was also separated from the others because they lived in the various valleys and plains and along the coast.

Most of the California Indians lived by hunting rabbits, deer, and waterfowl, and by fishing and gathering grasses, herbs, nuts, roots, seeds, berries, and insects. Their seed gathering was described by Mrs. Shirley Clappe, who came to the gold fields with her physician husband in 1850:

> We passed one place where a number of Indian women were gathering flower-seeds, which, mixed with pounded acorns and grasshoppers, forms the bread of these people. Each one carried two brown baskets woven with a neatness which is absolutely marvelous. . . .
>
> One of these queer baskets is suspended from the back and is kept in place by a thong of leather passing across the forehead. The other they carry in the right hand, and wave over the flower seeds with a motion as regular and monotonous as that of a mower. When they have collected a handful of these seeds, they pour them into the basket behind and continue this work until they have filled the latter with their strange harvest. It was very interesting to watch their regular motion, they seemed so exactly to keep time with each other and with their dark, shining skins, beautiful limbs and lithe forms, they were by no means the least picturesque feature of the landscape.

One of the staples of their diet was acorns, which they

made into flour for bread or porridge. These acorns had great nutritious value. The acorn was as important to these Indians as corn was to the Mexicans or wheat to our own culture. A common sound in Indian villages was that of the women pounding acorns with stone mortars to prepare acorn flour. Edward G. Buffum, a forty-niner, followed some Indian women to their camp and sampled some of their bread:

We followed in the direction which they had taken and soon reached the Indian rancheria. It was located on both sides of a deep ravine, across which was thrown a large log as a bridge, and consisted of about twenty circular wigwams, built of brush, plastered with mud, and capable of containing three or four persons. As we entered, we observed our flying beauties, seated on the ground, pounding acorns on a large rock. Pule-u-le explained that we were friends, and mentioned the high estimation in which I held them, which so pleased them, that one of the runaways left the wigwam and soon brought me a large piece of bread made of acorns, which to my taste was of a much more excellent flavor than musty hard bread.

A description of Indians netting sardines is given by Alfred Robinson, who arrived in California in 1829:

The Indians may be daily seen up to their knees in the surf, with their nets, which are easily filled and thus the inhabitants are supplied with provisions.

It is a merry sight, to behold on a bright sunny day, the joy of the Indians at the landing place, as they scoop with their nets—the leaping of the silvery fish that are thrown upon the rocks—the darting of the birds and the splashing of the water as they pounce upon their prey—the jumping porpoise—the spouting whale, all of which attract hundreds of spectators to the beach and keep them there for hours, beholders of the scene.

The Indians included in their diet certain roots and bulbs, but these were not their chief food. They were contemptuously named "Diggers" by the California- and Oregon-bound pioneers, who saw them digging in the ground with sticks and sneered at them because they had so little clothing and so few possessions.

Actually, the women were usually digging for root fibers which they used in basketry, rather than for food. Perhaps the term Digger was given to the Indians to degrade them, thus making it easier to justify taking away their land and lives. Before we can kill people, we have to learn to hate them. If we can portray people as miserable, treacherous, subhuman, and rob them of human dignity or pride, it is much easier to justify killing them and treating them worse than we would treat animals.

The California Indians hunted with bows and stone-tipped arrows and fished with nets, hooks, and harpoons. These, along with knives, were their only weapons. Their arrows were made with great skill and care. Buffum wrote that he had never seen "more beautiful specimens of workmanship."

The bows were three feet long, but very elastic and some of them were beautifully carved, and strung with intestines of birds. The arrows were about eighteen inches in length, accurately feathered and headed with a perfectly clear and transparent crystal, of a kind which I had never before seen, notched on the sides, and sharp

An Indian squaw pounding acorns, a sketch from Joseph Bruff's journal

as a needle at the point. The arrows, of which each Indian had at least twenty, were carried in a quiver made of coyote skin.

Seldom enjoying a surplus of food, the Indians carefully collected and stored all that they could obtain in baskets which were so skillfully made that it was unnecessary for them to develop the art of pottery. Their baskets were so tightly woven that they could hold water without calking. Some were decorated with woven-in feathers, beads, and shells. In addition to their being used for storage, baskets also served as cooking utensils and as plates and bowls for eating.

Their sanitary methods were ingenious and well suited to their culture. When their villages became too full of refuse and garbage, they set fire to their houses and moved on to new locations. They bathed frequently, and the use of the *temescal*, or sweathouse, was an important part of their society. Long before the sauna became a fad, the California Indians took sweat baths.

Their dwellings varied from redwood lodges to conical or dome-shaped huts built partially underground and banked with dirt. The coastal Indians built rafts of rushes, redwood dugouts, and canoes made of planks tightly joined together.

They dressed according to their mild climate. The men usually went naked or wore a loincloth, while the women wore a short, two-piece skirt made of plant fibers. Most of the Indians had a knowledge of herbs and natural remedies. Colton relates their skillful application to a young friend of his who "had been several months in Monterey, confined to his room, and nearly helpless from an ugly sore on one of his limbs."

California Indians dancing and bathing after a sweat bath,
sketched by J. W. Revere, U.S.N., 1849

The skill of the whole medical profession here, in the army and navy, and out of them, had been exerted in this case, and baffled. At last, the discouraged patient sent for an old Indian woman, who had some reputation among the natives for medical sagacity in roots and herbs. She examined the sore, and the next day brought the patient a poultice and pot of tea. The applications were made and the beverage drank as directed. These were renewed two or three times, and the young man is now running about the streets, or hunting his game, sound as a nut.

In California Indian life, the family was the most important institution, and friendship was valued highly. Delano's store was near an Indian village. Over a period of three months he made frequent visits to the *rancheria*. He reports, "I was soon looked upon as a friend."

It has been supposed that they are taciturn in their dispositions. This may be so in their intercourse with whites and others with whom they are not acquainted; but among themselves, and with those in whom they can confide, a more jolly, laughter-loving, careless and good natured people do not exist. The air resounded with their merry shouts as we sat around their fires at night, when some practical joke was perpetrated, or funny allusion made. And they were always ready to dance or sing at the slightest intimation, and nothing seemed to give them more pleasure than to have me join them in their recreation. To each other they were uniformly kind, and during the whole of my residence with them, I never saw a quarrel or serious disagreement.

Children were desired and welcomed and loved by

their parents. A woman was carefully treated during childbirth and afterward kept in bed and on a special diet until she regained her strength. She was cared for by her mother or another older woman and by her husband. Babies were carried bound to a board made of sticks and deerskin on their mothers' backs, until they were old enough to stand and walk.

Marriage was an informal ceremony. Funeral rites were much more elaborate, some tribes burying their dead, others cremating them. Delano tells the story of two young Indians who went to work and live with a rancher, Mr. Johnson. He became fond of them and raised them practically as his own children. When they were of age, they married each other; but in a year or two, the boy sickened and died.

Mr. Johnson intended to bury the body in a beautiful spot on his farm. But the poor girl begged him to let her lay her beloved husband besides the bones of his father in the hills. Of course, he consented, and when all was ready, set out, accompanied by his guests and retainers, to escort the body to the mountains. They were met by the rude mountaineers, with every demonstration of sorrow, who placed the body on a pile and set fire to it. As it was consuming, the Indians began to dance around it with slow and measured tread, accompanied with songs of lamentation, and casting into the flames some precious offering, while the widow stripped herself completely of her civilized garments, and threw them into the fire. When all was consumed, the Indians gathered up the ashes in their hands, and scattered them to the winds.

After the ceremony, Mr. Johnson told the young widow that her mule was ready, and they would return, but she refused to go. "My husband, my heart, is dead; I will stay in the mountains with him; I will watch his ashes on the hills, and his spirit shall be with me. I am an Indian now. I love you, my father, but I will go no more to the valley. I will be an Indian till I die."

The life of the California Indian was hard but satisfying. For everything there was a season and a time. Life had a pattern. It was complete and full and shared with family, friends, and tribe.

Because of the necessity to live on the limited plant and animal food available to them, the California Indians lived in small settled communities, or *rancherias*, of about 100 to 500 people. Socially and economically self-sufficient, they tended to stay mainly in their own locality and to do little traveling. Independent languages and dialects grew up. There were over 135 different tribes, mainly linguistic groups. The California Indians were never united as were the eastern and Plains Indians into strong military and nationalist groups and alliances.

To the Spanish, the name "California" represented *El Dorado*, "the Gilded." It was taken from a Spanish romance, *Las Sergias de Esplandian*, written by Garcia Ordoñez de Montalvo in Seville in 1510. His novel mentioned a rich island of California "on the right hand of the Indies, very near the Terrestrial Paradise," peopled with black Amazons, griffins, and other creatures of the author's imagination. The Amazons' weapons were of gold, "for in all the island there was no other metal." His book was very popular among the conquistadors at the time when Baja California was discovered.

But instead of gold, silver, jewels, silk, and spices, the early Spanish explorers found a barren, stormswept coast and tribes of poor Indian fishermen. The farthest away and the most isolated of her New World possessions, California was the least important colony to the Spanish. California was comparable to a distant Roman outpost in the days of the Empire; she was on the periphery of Spain's holdings in the New World.

It wasn't until 1765, when the British and Russians took an interest in the fur trade of the Pacific Coast, that the Spanish launched their first real attempt to populate California. Hand in hand with the military, the Franciscan friars were sent to build missions along the coast where the Indians could be "civilized" and trained to cultivate the land for their Spanish majesties and the glory of God. The Spanish attitude toward the Indians was more similar to that of the French than that of the English. The Spaniards recognized the Indians as human beings, permitted intermarriage with them, and believed in their assimilation into the Spanish culture as full-fledged Spanish citizens. But the Spaniards forced the Indians to work for them and often exploited them cruelly. The most tragic effect of the Indians' contact with the Spanish was their exposure to European diseases. Syphilis ran riot in California in 1776, causing death and crippling thousands of Indians at the missions. They had no immunity to certain diseases, or knowledge of how to combat them. Dysentery, smallpox, malaria, measles, and pleurisy decimated the ranks of the coastal Indians.

At the missions, the Indians were taught to plant, farm, and irrigate the land. They also became skilled in weaving, pottery, blacksmithing, shoemaking, and other occupations. At the *ranchos*, the Indians were taught to ride, herd, and look after horses and cattle.

Between 1769 and 1823, twenty-one missions were established between San Diego and San Francisco. Few Spanish colonists from Mexico were attracted to this far-off, empty land, so the population consisted mainly of soldiers, their families, missionaries, and their Indian converts. Spain's contact with the Indians was limited to the coastal tribes.

In 1822 there were about three thousand Spaniards in all of California. They lived mainly along the coast in their towns, forts, and *ranchos*, and had limited information about the interior and the great Central valley. Having little interest in Mexico's quarrel with the mother country, Californians hardly felt the change when Mexico became independent of Spain in 1822.

In 1834 the missions were secularized. Land, cattle, and orchards gradually ended up in the hands of merchants, speculators, and *rancheros*. The Indians, as trained vaqueros and farmers, became a cheap, useful labor force for the Spanish Californians. Many Indians took jobs as servants or did other menial labor; some fled into the Great Valley, to live with the Indian tribes there.

The Indian did most of the hard physical labor in California, and his condition was practically that of a slave. An Indian who was in debt to his master could not leave until the debt was paid. On quitting service, the laborer had to get a paper from his late employer, showing that he was properly discharged. Native laborers were not allowed to move about without a permit and were usually paid whatever their masters chose to give them. Robinson commented:

They had worked and been trained in the Missions and also worked upon the rancheros and for the towns-

people. *Skilled workers, the white settlers depended upon them, and they made possible the pastoral age and the leisurely life of the Mexicans.*

The main industry of the area was cattle raising, and the chief products were tallow and hides for export. Mining, lumbering, and manufacturing were largely unknown.

The United States' interest in California began in the 1780s when New England whalers hunted sea otters and seals for their fur, which they sold in China. The number of these mammals off the California coast seemed inexhaustible. They were slaughtered unmercifully, until by the 1820s they had all but disappeared. Then the whalers were replaced by New England merchant ships that came with cargoes of Yankee manufactured goods which they traded for hides and tallow.

The best description of this trade and of the California of the 1830s is by Richard Henry Dana. After a severe case of measles had temporarily affected his eyesight, Dana left Harvard to try and regain his health. He shipped off to sea as a common sailor for two years aboard the Boston brig *Plymouth*, which was engaged in the hide trade along the California coast. Dana's journal was later published under the title *Two Years Before the Mast.*

When the *Plymouth* arrived off California, people flocked out to the boat to examine the goods she had brought:

We began trading. For a week or ten days all was life on board. The people came off to look and to buy—men, women and children, and we were continually going in the boats, carrying goods and passengers,—for they have no boats of their own. Everything must dress itself and come aboard and see the new vessel, if it were only to buy a paper of pins. Our cargo was an assorted one: that is, it consisted of everything under the sun. We had spirits of all kinds, teas, coffee, sugar, spices, raisins, molasses, hardware, crockery-ware, tin-ware, cutlery, clothing of all kinds, boots and shoes from Lynn, calicoes and cotton from Lowell, crapes, silks; also shawls, scarfs, necklaces, jewelry and combs for the women; furniture and in fact, everything that can be imagined from Chinese fireworks to English cartwheels.

A typical son of the industrious, productive New England area, Dana could not understand the failure of the Californians to be actively engaged in industry.

The Californians are an idle, thriftless people and can make nothing for themselves. The country abounds in grapes, yet they buy at a great price, bad wines made in Boston and brought round by us. Their hides, too, which they value at two dollars in money, they barter for something which costs seventy-five cents in Boston, and buy shoes (as like as not made of their own hides which have been carried round Cape Horn) at three and four dollars, and "chicken-skin boots" at fifteen dollars a pair. Things sell, on the average, at an advance of nearly three hundred per cent upon the Boston prices.

Since there were so many cattle in California, there was no market for the beef. The vaqueros, the California cowboys, drove the cattle down to the seacoast. There they slaughtered them and staked their hides to dry. The fat was melted down into tallow in large iron kettles. Bags, or *botas*, were made from some of the whole hides, and the tallow was poured into them. The hides and *botas* were stored in huts until the arrival of one of the New England trading vessels which brought them back to the factories of Boston and the eastern cities.

Along with cattle, horses flourished and multiplied in this natural grazing land. They were so numerous that they were allowed to graze freely, the lassoes around their necks dragging on the ground so that anyone could catch and ride them. Horsemanship was the mark of the true Californian, and not to ride well was considered a disgrace. Colton claimed that the Californian was born, lived, and died in the saddle.

The moment a child is born on a farm in California, and the nurse has had time to dress it, it is given to a man on horseback, who with its future godfather and godmother, ride post-haste with it to some mission, and present it to a priest for baptism. This ceremony concluded, the party, full of glee, start on their return; and the little newcomer may now, perhaps, rest a week or two, before he starts on another excursion; but after that hardly a day will elapse without his being on horseback. He literally rides from his cradle to his grave.

His clothing, equipment, personal possessions—all were affected by his being a horseman. The Mexican and Californian vaquero was the true forerunner of our American cowboy. "His horse seldom trots," wrote Colton, "and will gallop all day without seeming to be weary. On his back is the Californian's home. Leave him this home, and you may have the rest of the world."

Soil and climate were so provident that a minimum amount of work was necessary for crops to grow. Beef, beans, and tortillas were the mainstays of the people's diet, and nearly all dishes were highly seasoned with peppers and garlic. Milk and dairy products were unknown, despite the hundreds of thousands of cows.

Work was not the main concern of the Californian, and no chance was overlooked in the pursuit of recreation and pleasure. Dancing was a passion of every Californian; two or three days were barely sufficient for celebrating weddings, parties, and balls. Any excuse was seized upon by the people as a chance to have a gathering and to enjoy themselves. The dance hall, reported Colton, "springs nightly to the step of those who are often greeted in the whirl of their amusement by the rising sun."

You might as well attempt to extinguish a love of air in a life preserver, as the dancing propensity in these people.

A Californian would have pause in a dance for an earthquake, and would be pretty sure to renew it, even before the vibrations had ceased. At a wedding they dance for three days and nights, during which time the new-married couple are kept on their feet. No compassion is shown them, as they have so much bliss in reserve.

As there were few inns or hotels, hospitality was freely extended to all travelers. This was an outstanding virtue of the Californian character. Writes Bancroft:

They possessed virtues worthy of record. They were kindhearted and liberal; a person could travel from San Diego to Sonoma without a coin in his pocket and never want for a roof to cover him, a bed to sleep on, food to eat, and even tobacco to smoke.

Serrano says in traveling, he once came to the house of

some poor people who had but one bed; this they wanted to give him, and sleep themselves on hides spread on the ground. The guest resisted, until they considered themselves slighted, and he was forced to yield. This hospitality was not only extended to acquaintances, but to strangers; and if any one attempted to pay for services rendered, the poorest Californian would never accept any reward and would say, "Senor, we are not in the habit of selling food."

Between 1825 and 1832, a small group of Americans settled in California and became leading merchants and traders in Santa Barbara, Los Angeles, and Monterey. Thomas Oliver Larkin settled in Monterey in 1832 and later became the American consul when the United States annexed California. Describing these businessmen, Dana writes:

In Monterey there are a number of English and Americans who have married Californians, become united to the Roman Church and acquired considerable property. Having more industry, frugality and enterprise than the natives, they soon get nearly all the trade into their hands. The people are naturally suspicious of foreigners, and they would not be allowed to remain, were it not that they conform to the Church, and by marrying natives and bringing up their children as Roman Catholics and Mexicans and not teaching them the English language, they quiet suspicion and even become leading and popular men. The chief Alcaldes in Monterey and Santa Barbara were Yankees by birth.

These, then, were the people and the culture that would be absorbed by the American takeover of California as a result of the Mexican-American War. For three years, Colton had enjoyed their hospitality, warmth, and friendship. He wrote with deep feelings of their society, which was about to change and disappear.

There are no people that I have ever been among who enjoy life so thoroughly as the Californians. Their habits are simple; their wants few; nature rolls almost everything spontaneously into their lap. They attach no value to money, except as it administers to their pleasures. A fortune, without the facilities of enjoying it, is with them no object of emulation or envy.

Their hospitality knows no bounds; they are always glad to see you, come when you may; take a pleasure in entertaining you while you remain; and only regret that your business calls you away. If you are sick, there is nothing which sympathy and care can devise or perform which is not done for you. If I must be cast in sickness or destitution on the care of strangers, let it be in California; but let it be before American avarice has hardened the heart and made a god of gold.

Mexican California was far from an ideal society; it had many faults and weaknesses. The great majority of the people barely eked out a living. Even for the landed, ruling class, the *rancheros*, with all their acres, cattle, horses, costumes, and love of life and celebration, life was hard. Isolated from the rest of the world, they were at the mercy of events they could not control and did not know how to handle. Upon this rural society, and upon the California Indians, was to burst the full impact of the gold rush, burying both cultures beyond recall.

LIFE IN THE DIGGINGS AND THE MINING CAMPS

Having arrived in San Francisco, the forty-niners hurriedly made their way up the Sacramento River to Sacramento City. From there, they headed for the diggings by means of stagecoach, horseback, mule, or on foot. The newcomers joined the miners already there or established new camps. The ring of pick and shovel striking rock; the swish of the cradle and pan; the shouts, curses, and songs of the argonauts filled the once quiet countryside.

Taught by old-timers how to pan, the new miner dug up a quantity of what he hoped was gold-bearing dirt and sand. Dumping this mixture into Indian baskets, tin cups, old hats, or blankets, he added a steady stream of water "to wash out the dirt." The gold, being heavier, would settle to the bottom while the loose dirt would float off with the water. Panning required patience, skill, and much physical exertion. Usually a man had to stoop or squat near a stream's edge, constantly shaking and rotating the pan, and at the same time picking out large stones and adding more water. "Panning is to the beginner," wrote George Payson, "a very curious and mysterious operation."

Panning for gold

I did as I was told, whirling and dipping with all my might. There was nothing in the appearance of the earth to distinguish it from what I had seen a thousand times at home. Yet this was the earth I had come twenty thousand miles to seek, and in that earth, there lurked, so I was told, and so I partly believed, the divers grains of gold.

Although not as thorough as panning, rocking was faster and became popular with the miners. A "rocker," or "cradle," was similar to a baby's cradle. Essentially it was a wooden box mounted on rockers and open at its lower end with a coarse grate or sieve at its head. Cleats, or "riffles," were nailed across the bottom to catch the gold. Three or more men worked the rocker, digging the dirt and supplying the buckets. This, too, was hard work, commented Daniel Woods, a forty-niner from Philadelphia:

I have been seated for several hours by the riverside, rocking a heavy cradle filled with dirt and stones. The person rocking the cradle with his left hand, at the same time uses his right in dipping up continually ladles of water which he dashes upon the dirt in the hopper. Twenty-five buckets of dirt are generally washed through.

The next step was the "Long Tom." This was a rocker lengthened into a trough. The Long Tom needed a steady stream of water, and two or three men were required to run it. It was no more efficient than the rocker, but the men could wash more dirt in the same period of time. The forty-niners also began digging ditches and draining streams to bring water to the dirt rather than the dirt to the water.

No matter which method they used, few miners just

Photograph taken in Auburn Ravine, 1852, showing a Long Tom

stumbled over gold. It was a highly intense business, requiring exacting work and systematic searching. All your energy and attention, said Johnson, was absorbed by your work:

At the edge of the stream, or knee deep and waist deep in water as cold as melted ice and snow, some were washing gold while the rays of the sun were pouring down upon their heads with an intensity exceeding anything we ever experienced at home.

The thirst for gold and the labor of acquisition overruled all else, and totally absorbed every faculty, complete silence reigned among the miners; they addressed not a word to each other, and seemed adverse to all conversation. All the sympathies of our common humanity, all the finer and nobler attributes of our nature seemed lost, buried beneath the soil they were eagerly delving, or swept away with the rushing waters that revealed the shining treasure.

The forty-niners were a restless breed of men. If they did not find gold right away, or enough of it, they would immediately leave for another point and try there. The merest rumor of a possible strike would send the miners scrambling over ridges and hills to the promised spot. There was a mania for rushes; whole camps stampeded, wrote Payson, illuminating such a scene:

The whole of the mining region was in a ferment. An ant-hill, just disturbed by some sudden alarm—a crowded steamboat, on the point of starting—afford apt illustrations of the frenzy that now invaded the entire population. Parties of miners flowed by in a continuous current. All seemed bent on some urgent business.

Everyone was afraid he should be too late—that he should not go to the richest placers—that he should not find the fortune intended for him—that he shouldn't be able to return home the coming winter—in short, that he should not improve the present golden opportunity to the very utmost.

Mining towns were very cosmopolitan, yet two-thirds of the miners were Americans. The miners were mostly young men. As with the cowboy and the shantyboy, men were rarely known or called by their full name. Most were called by nicknames. There was Red Rover, Dutch Jake, Yankee Jimmy, Sailor Jack, Fuzzy, Hatchet, and Hell-Roaring Jo. One man who always got lost while prospecting was called Compass. A fancy dresser was named Frippery Jim; a deacon, Pious Pete. It was not healthy or polite to inquire too closely into a man's background unless he volunteered it. A popular little ditty in the gold fields was this simple verse which greeted newcomers to the diggings:

> Oh, what was your name in the States?
> Was it Thompson, or Johnson or Bates?
> Did you flee for your life or murder your wife?
> Say, what was your name in the States?

The miners dressed in various styles and hues. Eastern clothes, top hat and overcoat, deerskin breeches, sombreros and bandanas—all were seen in the mines. Many forty-niners wore flannel shirts, mainly of red and blue. Woolen pantaloons were usually tucked into their high boot tops. Almost everybody wore boots because they were constantly wading in and out of water. They preferred clothes that hid the dirt and washed easily. A low-crowned, broad-brimmed soft wool or felt hat completed the outfit.

The mining towns themselves were composed mainly of tents and rough log or bark structures. They were usually found at the bottom of deep riverbeds and ravines. The appearance of the towns was as rough and uncivilized as that of the forty-niners who lived and worked in them. A British artist, J. D. Borthwick, who visited several mining towns, described the town of Placerville, or "Hangtown" as it was called: "It consisted of one, long straggling street of clapboard houses and log cabins, built in a hollow at the side of a creek, and surrounded by high and steep hills."

Even the main street, muddy and broken up, was not exempt from prospectors digging for gold. Relates Borthwick:

Here and there, in the middle of the street, was a square hole, about six feet deep, in which one miner was digging, while another was bailing the water out with a bucket, and a third, sitting alongside the heap of dirt which had been dug up, was washing it in a rocker.

The names of the mining towns were no less colorful and descriptive than the names of the miners themselves: Poker Flat, Humbug Canyon, Poverty Hill, You Bet, Squabbletown, Chucklehead Diggings, Git Up and Git, and Mad Ox Ravine. Towns were constantly thrown up as new strikes were made; they died as quickly when their gold finds were exhausted and the miners moved to new diggings.

Boardinghouses, restaurants, saloons, gambling houses, houses of prostitution, and stores nestled one next to the

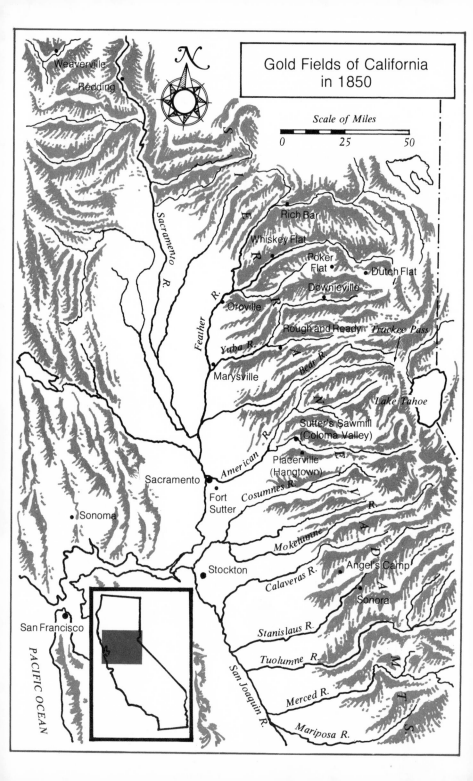

other, all existing to service the miners and his needs and to part him from his gold. Storekeepers set up flimsy tents or crude shacks. Goods were expensive because they had to be transported from San Francisco to the gold fields. In addition, there were shortages of everything in the mining camps, so the merchants could set their own prices, frequently double and triple what the same goods would cost in San Francisco or Sacramento.

Money seemed to have absolutely no value to the miners. They spent their gold dust recklessly. If they had worked hard for it, they felt they owed themselves a treat; if they had found it easily, they were certain they could always get more. Champagne, cordials and choice liquors, oysters and other luxuries were bought freely by the miners when they felt flushed. One forty-niner, A. J. McCall, told how the miners were always ready to celebrate and go on a "bust":

Bill Lucre and Gus Miller were roving, reckless characters, always ready for a "bust." Once in paying for something, Bill dropped a small piece of gold, which a bystander picked up and offered to him. Without taking it he looked at the finder, with a comical mixture of scorn and amazement, and broke out,

"Well, stranger, you are a curiosity. You haven't been in the diggings long; better keep it for a sample."

At another time they purchased a barrel of ale at $10 per bottle, and sardines at a half ounce per box; and with a bottle under each arm and glass in hand, they went about among a crowd at Coloma, forcing everybody to eat and drink.

Molasses cost $1 per bottle; vinegar the same. Melons were $2 to $5 apiece; flour sold for as much as $1 a pound; a single potato or onion cost $1. A pair of coarse boots brought $16; good boots were $50 or more. A frying pan was $6, a coffee pot $10; and knives and forks were $20 a dozen. A single candle could cost $1.25, and rope was $2.25 a pound. A wool hat cost $12 and a comb $2. Ink was $4 a bottle—no wonder the miners seldom wrote home.

Thus as fast as the miners made money, they had to exchange it for necessities. Bancroft commented: "It was the diggers alone who produced the gold; as for the rest, all preyed on them and on each other."

The miners resented the fact that while they did the hard work, the storekeepers, gamblers, and speculators made the profits. Hiram Pierce, a forty-niner, expressed the feelings of many in the diggings when he commented: "Many are making great fortunes in a little time, but they do not make it by digging. It is by trading and speculating."

Yet the storekeepers ran great risks and often lost all. Since miners were constantly arriving and moving on as soon as a new strike was found, the population of the mining towns flowed and ebbed. The storekeepers had to buy their goods at inflated prices from San Francisco or Sacramento and trust that they could sell them. The huge additional cost of freighting goods to the mines added to their overhead. To maintain business and keep the goodwill of the miners, the merchants often sold on credit. The miners were mainly honest men, but if their diggings did not pan out, there was no way they could pay for their supplies; the storekeeper just had to write off their debts.

Miners shopped once a week for food. Flour and salt pork were their staples. Other essentials were beans, rice,

Trading a pan of beans for a pan of gold, 1849 cartoon

bacon, dried apples, coffee, sugar, molasses, and saleratus or baking soda for their bread. Occasionally fresh meat could be had, supplied by drovers who brought in herds of cattle or hogs from San Francisco. Hunters sold the game they killed—bear, deer, elk, or rabbit. The only trouble with fresh meat was that it spoiled so quickly; salt meat, which lasted a long time, was preferred.

The miners' bill of fare did not vary much from one meal to the next. Their gear was of the simplest. Frequently, three or four miners lived together and divided up the domestic work. They took turns cooking, chopping wood, making fires, carrying water, and other chores. They lived as simply as they could. Says Woods:

An iron pan, which we use for washing gold, serves also for boiling our coffee. A frying-pan is our only cooking utensil. In this one of the company fries some pork which is rancid, and then, in the fat, fries some flour batter. After it is done on one side, he tosses it whirling up, catching it as it comes down upon the other side, which is then fried in turn. A spade answers very well for a plate. We use coffee without sugar, bread without salt, salad without vinegar.

Tobacco was a necessity and a comfort for the miners. In one camp, there was only one pipe for eight smokers. It made the rounds, everyone taking his turn.

The mining season was limited by heat, cold, snow, and rain. The best mining months were April, May, June, October, and November. In the summer, miners worked an eight-hour day, resting between 11 A.M. and 4 P.M., when the heat was unbearable. Some days it was so hot they could not work at all. Yet the nights were chilly and the men needed blankets.

A domestic chore in the mining camp

Miners weighing their gold

Rain began around the end of November or the beginning of December. From then on, it fell constantly, usually through March. Placers were underwater, and the holes the miners dug collapsed. Isolated in the primitive camps by floods, the miners led a melancholy existence. Worse, they made no money. Most of the gold-seekers moved to the larger towns of Coloma, Sacramento, or San Francisco for the winter. In the spring, they returned to the diggings. Those who stayed in the mines year round were usually broke and had no other choice.

The majority of miners were far from healthy. They spent little time taking care of themselves. Housed inadequately, many slept on the ground, and few rested properly. Woods' diary of July 10, 1849, has this entry:

We made $3 each today. This life of severe hardship and exposure has affected my health. Our diet consisted of hard bread, flour, which we eat half cooked and salt pork, with occasionally a salmon which we purchase off the Indians. Vegetables are not to be procured. Our feet are wet all day, while a hot sun shines down upon our heads, and the very air parches the skin like the hot air of an oven. Our drinking water comes down to us thoroughly impregnated with the mineral substances washed through the thousand cradles above us.

Even when they were not working, the miners could not completely relax. Always under pressure, they were eager to strike it rich and repay themselves for all the hardships they had endured. Caught in the squeeze of high prices and scarcity of goods, they always had to eat and buy provisions, whether they found gold or not. No matter how hard they worked, many just managed to break even, and a great number were perpetually in debt. Woods' journal entry of January 15 reads:

This morning, notwithstanding the rain, we were again at our work. We must work. In sunshine and rain, in warm and cold, in sickness and health, successful or not successful, early and late, it is work, work, WORK! Work or perish! All around us, above and below, on mountain side and stream, the rain falling fast upon them are the miners at work—not for gold, but for bread. Lawyers, doctors, clergymen, farmers, soldiers, deserters, good and bad, from England, from America, from China, from the Islands, from every country—all, all at work, at their cradles. From morning to night is heard the incessant rock, rock, rock.

Sickness was prevalent in the diggings. The forty-niners suffered from back trouble, sore hands and feet, dysentery, rheumatism, malaria, diarrhea, ague, chills and fevers, and pulmonary troubles. Scurvey was common because the miners lived on salt and pickled meat, without any fresh vegetables. Miners seldom had time to wash themselves or cut their hair. They had a running battle with their constant companions: vermin, fleas, and lice.

There was little hope of getting adequate medical care. While doctors were available, both they and the medicines they prescribed were terribly expensive. Few miners could afford repeated visits to the doctor. C. Fay, an argonaut, wrote with tongue in cheek: "The Doctors charge pretty well. They charge for pills as if they were diamonds, and bleed a man of an ounce of gold and an ounce of blood at the same time."

A sick man was lucky if he had comrades who might

attend to him, but many were without friends. Worn out and alone, many did not make a fight against disease. Dr. Stillman and his associates built a free hospital in Sacramento City. Writing home, Stillman told of the sick and destitute miners. He had counted 800 graves on the outskirts of the city in the rude cemetery:

Men in the ravings of delirium, call upon friends who are far off, and dying, mutter the names of their loved ones; men wasting away with chronic disease, lose their manhood, and weep often, like children, to see their mothers once more.

When a forty-niner died, he was usually wrapped in his blanket and a deep hole dug. Burial services were short and simple; and as soon as they were over, the miners hurried back to their diggings to make up for lost time. Even death could not interrupt the endless search for gold. Marryat relates how digging a grave turned into digging for gold:

One of the miners died, and having been much respected, it was determined to give him a regular funeral. The grave had been dug at a distance of a hundred yards from the camp. The minister commenced with an extempore prayer, during which all knelt round the grave.

The prayer was unnecessarily long, and some of the mourners began absentmindedly fingering the loose earth thrown up from the grave.

It was thick with gold; and an excitement was immediately apparent in the kneeling crowd. The preacher stopped, and inquiringly said, "Boys, what's that? Gold!" he continued, "and the richest kind—the congregation are dismissed!" The poor miner was taken from his grave and was buried elsewhere, while the funeral party, with the parson at their head, lost no time in prospecting the new diggings.

Yet, with all their hardships, the forty-niners did take time out to play. Wrestling matches, jumping matches, other athletic contests, bull and bear fights, story-telling, and tall tales helped them pass the time. There was much horseplay and practical jokes.

During the week, many mining towns were comparatively quiet. On Sundays, miners from eight to ten miles around flocked in. Some came to buy provisions; others to drink, gamble, and play cards; still others to get their mail. After a week's hard labor, though, most made the journey to enjoy themselves. Recalled C. W. Gillespie:

The principal street of Coloma was alive with crowds of moving men, laughing, talking, and all appearing in the best of humor.

The street was one continuous din. Thimble-riggers, French monte dealers, or string-game tricksters were shouting aloud at every corner: "Six ounces, gentlemen, no one can tell where the little joker is!" or "Bet on the jack, the jack's the winning card! Three ounces no man can turn up the jack!" or "Here's the place to git your money back! The veritable string game! Here it goes! There, six, twelve ounces no one can put his finger in the loop!"

As time went on, stagecoaches brought in professional entertainers and actors. Shakespeare, vaudeville acts, minstrel shows, circuses, and concerts were presented to the miners. Starved for entertainment, they formed appreciative audiences.

The miners liked to sing. Miners' songs were varied, ranging from the comic to the tragic. Parodies of popular songs were especially common. "Joe Bowers" was one of the best-known of the goldmining songs.

Joe Bowers

My name it is Joe Bow - ers, I've got a bro- ther Ike, I'm just here from Mis - sou - ri and

all   the   way   from   Pike;   I'll

tell   you   why   I   left   there   and

why   I   came   to   roam,   And

leave   my   ag - ed   par - ents   so

far a - way from home.

My name it is Joe Bowers, I've got a brother Ike,
I'm just here from Missouri and all the way from Pike;
I'll tell you why I left there and why I came to roam,
And leave my aged parents so far away from home.

I used to court a girl there, her name was Sally Black,
I asked her if she'd marry, she said it was a whack;
Says she to me, "Joe Bowers, before we're hitched for life,
You ought to get a little home to keep your little wife."

Says I, "My dearest Sally, oh Sally for your sake,
I'll go to California and try to raise a stake";
Says she to me, "Joe Bowers, you're just the one to win,"
She gave me a kiss to seal the bargain, and throwed a dozen in.

At last I went to mining, put in my biggest licks,
Came down upon the boulders just like a thousand bricks;
I worked both late and early, in rain, in sun and snow,
I was working for my Sally, 'twas all the same to Joe.

One day I got a letter from my dear brother Ike,
It came from old Missouri, all the way from Pike,
It brought me the darndest news that ever you did hear,
My heart it is a-breaking, so please excuse this tear.

It said my Sal was false to me, that her love for me had fled,
That she had got married to a butcher whose hair was red;
It told me more than that, it's enough to make me swear,
That Sal had had a baby and the baby had red hair.

Anyone who could play an instrument—a guitar, banjo, harmonica, or accordion—was always welcomed and treated to drinks. Frequently dances were held, even though there were no women present. Borthwick describes one such "ball":

It was a strange sight to see a party of long bearded men, in heavy boots and flannel shirts, going through all the steps and figures of the dance with so much spirit, and often with a great deal of grace, hearty enjoyment depicted on their dried-up sunburned faces, and revolvers and bowie-knives glancing in their belts; while a crowd of the same rough-looking customers stood around, cheering them on to greater efforts, and occasionally dancing a step or two quietly on their own account.

The absence of ladies was a difficulty which was very easily overcome; it was understood that every gentleman who had a patch on a certain part of his inexpressibles should be considered a lady for the time being.

In the early days of the gold rush, few women were found in the mines or the mining towns. Traveling to the diggings was too hard and living conditions too unsettled for women to live there. The miners felt keenly the lack of women and of female companionship and daydreamed of their wives and families back home. One forty-niner, Thissell, recalls how he heard the news that a white woman had come to Snow's Camp:

Next morning I put on my best jeanpants, a pair of alligator boots, a red flannel shirt, my old wool hat lopped down over my ears. I struck out on foot to see the wonderful creature. When I arrive in Snow's Camp, it was

A miners' ball

late in the day and Mrs. Snow kept a restaurant. I ordered dinner at $1.50. While eating, I saw some eggs in a pan. On inquiry, I learned they were worth one dollar each, so I ordered one cooked. This brought my dinner up to $2.50.

It was dark long before I reached home, and should I live to be a hundred—I shall never forget the day I walked 16 miles to see a woman in California.

By 1850 women were arriving in San Francisco and going out to the mining towns. "Shirley" Amelia Clappe had come from New England with her physician husband, Fayette Clappe. She wrote a series of letters to her sister back in New England, which were published as "The Shirley Letters" serially in a San Francisco periodical, *The Pioneer*. After a year in San Francisco, the doctor moved his practice to the diggings at Rich Bar, a small camp on the Feather River. Opening his office there, he sent for his wife to join him. Shirley tells how "my numerous acquaintances in San Francisco rained one universal shout of disapprobation":

Some said that I ought to be in a strait jacket, for I was undoubtedly mad to think of such a thing, some said that I should never get there alive, and if I did would not stay a month—that even if the Indians did not kill me, I should expire of ennui or the cold before spring. One lady declared in a burst of outraged modesty that it was absolutely indelicate, to think of living in such a large population of men; where at the most there were but two or three women.

"I laughed merrily," commented Shirley, "and started gaily to commence my journey to Rich Bar."

At first the Clappes stayed at the Empire, "the only two-storied building in town." The landlady of the Empire, relates Shirley, "was Mrs. B.";

a gentle and amiable looking woman, about twenty-five years of age. She is an example of the terrible wear and tear to the complexion in crossing the plains, here having become, through exposure at that time, of a dark and permanent yellow. She took a nursing babe of eight months old from her bosom, and left it with two other children, almost infants—to cross the plains in search of gold! When I arrived, she was cooking supper for some half-a-dozen people.

In addition there was Mr. and Mrs. Bailey who had three pretty children and lived at the entrance to the village in a log cabin. Scarcely a week later, Shirley's next letter told of the death of poor Mrs. Bailey who "died of peritonitis (a common disease in the camps) after an illness of four days only!"

In October the Clappes moved to a log cabin in the nearby community of Indian Bar. After describing the primitive cabin to her sister, Shirley commented:

How would you like to winter in such an abode? In a place where there are no newspapers, no churches, lectures, concerts, or theaters; no fresh books, no shopping, calling, nor gossiping, little tea-drinkings; no parties, no balls, no picnics, no latest fashions, no daily mail, no promenades, no rides; no vegetables but potatoes and onions, no milk, no eggs, no nothing?

Delighted to be in her own home, Shirley optimistically answered all her own questions: "I expect to be very happy here."

In September 1852 the Clappes made a journey to the American Valley. On their way they met many of the emigrants who had just come overland. Describing one such woman, "a widow whom we used to call the 'long woman,'" Shirley wrote:

When but a few weeks on the journey, she had buried her husband, who died of cholera after about six hours illness. She had come on, for what else could she do? No one was willing to guide her back to her old home in the States. She was living under a large tree and sleeping at night, with her whole family, in her one covered wagon.

This woman, a Mrs. Roger, had "nine small children and one at the breast." Continued Shirley:

She was immensely tall, and had a hard, weatherbeaten face, a heavy twist of hay-colored hair, which, before it was cut and its gloss all destroyed by the alkali, must have been very handsome. But what interested me so much in her, was the dogged and determined way in which she had set herself against poverty. She owned nothing in the world but her team, and yet she planned all sorts of successful ways to get food for her large family. She used to wash shirts and iron them on a chair. She made me think of a long-legged, very thin hen, scratching for dear life, to feed her never-to-be-satisfied brood.

On November 21, 1852, Shirley wrote her twenty-third and final letter. The diggings at Indian Bar and Rich Bar ended in failure, with the miners bankrupt. "Nearly all of the fluming companies had failed—contrary to every expectation, on arriving at the bed-rock, no gold made its appearance."

The failure of the miners affected the whole community.

The whole world (our world) was "dead broke." The shopkeepers, restaurants, and gambling houses had trusted the miners to that degree, that they themselves were in the same moneyless condition. Such a batch of woeful faces was never seen before, not the least elongated of which was F's, to whom nearly all the companies owed large sums.

It is said "that there are not twenty men remaining on Indian Bar, although two months ago, you could count them up by hundreds."

With his practice gone, the doctor prepared to move back to San Francisco. Shirley took leave of her mountain home in these plaintive words: "My heart is heavy at the thought of departing forever from this place. I *like* this wild and barbarous life; I leave it with regret."

Many young women came to California to find a husband for themselves. One young lady put an ad in a Marysville paper. She was possessed of both a good sense of humor and a lot of determination. There is little doubt that she must have gotten her man. Her ad ran:

A HUSBAND WANTED

BY A LADY who can wash, cook, scour, sew, milk, spin, weave, hoe, (can't plow), cut wood, make fires, feed the pigs, raise chickens, rock the cradle (gold-rocker, I thank you, Sir!), saw a plank, drive nails, etc., and as you can see, she can write.

Her age is none of your business. She is neither hand-

some nor a fright, yet an old man need not apply. There must be $20,000 settled on her, before she will bind herself.

Many miners dreamed of making their pile and returning home to marry their sweetheart. But no matter how strenuously a miner worked, he could not be sure of making any money. Hundreds of miners became disillusioned, left the diggings, and returned home. Some went to San Francisco or Sacramento and took jobs. Others stayed in the gold fields and worked for more successful miners.

Others kept on digging and hoping that someday they would strike it rich. Some men did make fantastic strikes. Most spent it as fast as they made it or lost it gambling or by investing in some crazy scheme. Every new find made those still prospecting confident that it would be their turn next. They lived on hope. But of the tens of thousands of miners who flocked to California few found the wealth they expected. Scores came with high hopes only to suffer the fate of one young miner, sketched by Woods, who died alone and unknown.

One young man near us has just died. He was without companion or friend—alone in his tent. Not even his name could be discovered. We buried him, tied down his tent, leaving his effects within.

That was the true epitaph of the gold rush.

The Lousy Miner

It's four long years since I reached this land, In search of gold among the rocks and sand; And yet I'm poor when the truth is told, I'm a lou - sy min - er,

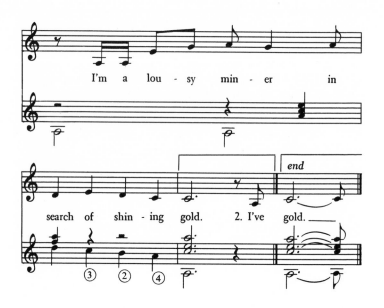

I'm a lou - sy min - er in search of shin - ing gold. 2. I've gold.

It's four long years since I reached this land,
In search of gold among the rocks and sand;
And yet I'm poor when the truth is told,
I'm a lousy miner,
I'm a lousy miner in search of shining gold.

I've lived on swine till I grunt and squeal,
No one can tell how my bowels feel,
With flapjacks swimming round in bacon grease.
I'm a lousy miner,
I'm a lousy miner; when will my troubles cease?

I was covered with lice coming on the boat,
I threw away my fancy swallow-tailed coat,
And now they crawl up and down my back;
I'm a lousy miner;
I'm a lousy miner, a pile is all I lack.

My sweetheart vowed, she would wait for me
Till I returned; but don't you see
She's married now, sure, so I'm told,
Left her lousy miner,
Left her lousy miner in search of shining gold.

Oh, land of gold, you did me deceive,
And I intend in thee my bones to leave;
So, farewell home; now my friends grow cold,
I'm a lousy miner
I'm a lousy miner in search of shining gold.

SAN FRANCISCO

Before the gold rush, San Francisco had been a sleepy little village consisting of a few huts scattered over a shady beach. With the opening of the gold fields, it became one of the fastest-growing cities in the world. Everything—merchandise, supplies, miners, and gold—had to come in and go out through this port. Here was the place where an enterprising fellow could make his pile—and a lot easier than in the diggings! Here, too, was the place where many forty-niners came in search of jobs or amusements, or to bank their gold, collect their mail, or board ship for the journey home.

San Francisco teemed with excitement. It was alive in every fiber of its being. It was crowded, dirty, a fire menace, growing without plan or direction. Business, building, selling, making money, seizing opportunities that are here today and may be gone tomorrow occupied everyone's attention. Observed Bayard Taylor:

Men dart hither and thither, as if possessed with a never-resting spirit. You speak to an acquaintance—a merchant, perhaps. He utters a few hurried words of greeting, while his eyes send keen glances on all sides of you; suddenly he catches sight of somebody in the crowd; he is off, and in the next five minutes has bought up half a cargo, sold a town lot at treble the sum he gave, and taken a share in some new and imposing speculation. The very air is pregnant with the magnetism of bold, spirited, unwearied action, and he who but ventures into the outer circle of the whirlpool is spinning in its dizzy vortex.

At first a sea of canvas tents and wooden shacks, San Francisco grew rapidly. The banging of hammers and the whining of saws could be heard from six o'clock in the morning till late at night. A correspondent for *Littell's Living Age* reported:

Verily the place was in itself a miracle. The rapidity with which a ready made house is put up and inhabited strikes the stranger in San Francisco as little short of magic. He walks over an open lot in a before breakfast stroll—the next morning a house complete with a family inside, blocks his way. He goes down to the bay and looks out on the shipping—two or three days afterwards a row of storage-houses, staring him in the face, intercepts the view.

Because of the numbers of wood and canvas houses, fire was an ever present danger, and fires were frequent. One of the worst fires broke out on May 3, 1851. It burned for ten hours, destroying twenty-two blocks and two thousand homes and much of the business district. Marryat describes the fire:

No conception can be formed of the grandeur of the scene for at one time the burning district was covered

A View of San Francisco, 1848

by one vast sheet of flame that extended half a mile in length. The shouts of the excited populace—the crash of falling timbers—the yells of the burnt and injured—the clank of the fire-brakes—the hoarse orders delivered through speaking trumpets—the maddened horses released from burning livery-stables plunging through the streets—helpless patients being carried from some hospital, and dying on the spot, as the swaying crowd, forced back by the flames, tramples all before it—explosion of houses blown up by gunpowder—showers of burning splinters that fall around on every side—the thunder of brick buildings as they fall into a heap of ruin—and the blinding flare of ignited spirits.

As fast as houses burned down, new ones were put up—before the ashes even stopped smoking. Gradually the wooden buildings were replaced by brick ones.

On the lot where I had observed the remains of gun-barrels and nails, stands its late proprietor, Mr. Jones, who is giving directions to a master-carpenter. The carpenter promises to get everything fixed right off, and have the store ready in two days. At this junction passes Mr. Smith, also in company with a cargo of building materials; he was the owner of the iron house; he says to Jones, interrogatively—

"Burnt out?"

Jones: "Yes, and burst up."

Smith: "Flat?"

Jones: "Flat, as a d——d pancake!"

Smith: "It's a great country."

Jones: "It's nothing shorter."

And in a couple of days both Smith and Jones are on

their legs again, and with a little help from their friends live to grow rich perhaps, and build brick buildings that withstand the flames.

Because of the scarcity of permanent buildings, lots and property went for astronomical figures. The price of houses and lots were from $10,000 to $75,000. Rents were enormous. A lawyer inquiring for a law office was shown a cellar in the earth and told he could rent it for $250 a month, cash down in advance.

Most of the streets had no sidewalks and were not paved. Mudholes were everywhere, some so deep as to make the streets impassable. Boxes, cases, trunks, all kinds of debris were thrown into these holes in an attempt to bridge them, but usually without success. Signs were put up warning travelers of the worst pitfalls: "Through passage to China." "Head of navigation, no bottom." "Horse and dray lost; look out for the soundings." "Office to let in the basement."

Rats infested the city. They came out at night; after dark, you had to kick them from the wooden sidewalks as you walked down the street. Cats sold for $16 each. Ratting dogs hunted down the rats, and crowds gathered to watch the dogs do their work. Burglaries were common after sunset, and men went armed in the unlighted streets at night.

The city swarmed with men: prospective forty-niners, new arrivals, used-up miners, farmers and workers. Borthwick sketches a picture of the French and Chinese miners arriving in San Francisco:

Troops of newly arrived Frenchmen marched along, enroute for the mines, staggering under their equipment

San Francisco street scene, the winter of 1849

of knapsacks, shovels, picks, tin wash-bowls, pistols, knives, swords, and double-barreled guns—their blankets slung over their shoulders, and their persons hung around with tin cups, frying-pans, coffee-pots, and other culinary utensils, with perhaps a hatchet and a spare pair of boots. Crowds of Chinamen were also to be seen, bound for the diggings, under gigantic basket-hats, each man with a bamboo laid across his shoulder, from each end of which was suspended a higgledy-piggledy collection of mining tools, Chinese baskets and boxes, immense boots and a variety of Chinese "fixins. . . ."

Labor was scarce in San Francisco and salaries high. Laundresses were heavily in demand and received $8 per dozen articles. Because of the scarcity of women to fill this profession, many ex-miners went into the business, reported Bayard Taylor, and found it much more profitable than the diggings:

It was an amusing sight to see a great, burly, long-bearded fellow kneeling on the ground, with sleeves rolled up to the elbows, and rubbing a shirt with such violence that the suds flew and the buttons, if there were any, must soon snap off. [Such men] succeeded fully as well as the women, and were rapidly growing rich from the profits of their business.

Others worked at the hundred and one different types of jobs available in the rapidly expanding city. Recalling his pioneer days in San Francisco, John Williamson Palmer left this list of activities:

They bustled and jostled, and tugged, and sweated, and made money—always made money. They labored and they lugged; they worked on lighters, drove trucks, packed mules, rang bells, carried messages, "waited" in restaurants, "marked" for billiard-tables, served drinks in barrooms, "faked" on the Plaza, "cried" at auctions, toted lumber for houses, ran a game of faro or roulette in the El Dorado or the Bella Union,—manipulated three-card monte on the head of a barrel in front of the Parker House; they speculated in beach and water-lots, in lumber, pork, flour, potatoes; in picks, shovels, pans, long boots, slouch hats, knives, blankets and Mexican saddles. There were doctors, lawyers, politicians, preachers, even gentlemen and scholars among them; but they all speculated, and as a rule they gambled.

More than balancing the high wages was the even higher cost of living. Baths cost $2 apiece. Water was very scarce; men were willing to pay 12½¢ for a bucketful. Food was expensive, and eating out was very dear. Yet, as with everything else in San Francisco, the numerous restaurants were always crowded.

Many men slept in lodging houses. These were usually long, barnlike tenements. They had no windows; along the sides were two rows of bunks, or wooden shelving. Men flocked in from about ten o'clock at night with their own blankets. Many preferred to sleep in the open air. Some even slept in pine coffins, just freshly built.

The streets of the city presented every variety of style in dress the world had seen for the last quarter of a century. "No man," wrote Bancroft, "could make his appearance sufficiently *bizarre* to attract any attention."

The men desperately longed for news, which was scarce in California. One enterprising forty-niner brought fifteen hundred copies of the New York *Tribune* along

Lining up at the post office, San Francisco, 1849

with him on the boat. He sold them within two hours after his arrival at $1 apiece.

Mail was one of the things that miners wanted most. Two or three times a month, mail steamers arrived. They brought the mail, newly arriving forty-niners, families from the East coming to join their argonaut husbands, adventurers and merchants, gamblers and cutthroats. When the steamship was sighted, a signal was unfurled on the windmill indicator on Telegraph Hill. A thrill went through the town. Wrote Bancroft:

Then a stream of hacks, and wagons and drays and men on foot, hotel-runners, working men, business men and loafers set in toward the wharf. Proudly the great ship sweeps around the bay to the city front. As she drops into her berth, the crowds on ship and shore begin their noisy jests and salutations. Some are there to meet their friends, others from curiosity; some have climbed from small boats up the side of the vessel while she was approaching the wharf; others stand on the tops of piers, and when the ship is within a few feet leap onto the deck, where there is a scene of embracing, kissing, laughing and crying, impossible to describe.

Since there were no postmen in San Francisco, the men had to go themselves to get their mail at the post office. There were half a dozen windows lettered A to E, F to K, and so on. Lines began to form at these windows as soon as the ship was sighted, although it might be twenty hours before the mail was ready for delivery. Everyone was orderly and took their turn. The lines were so long that a wait of six hours was not unusual. Some men came with books and newspapers to read. A man's place in line

The bar of a San Francisco gambling saloon

was his individual property, and he could sell it. Some men lined up early just to sell their place to someone with money and no time. A good position would bring $10 to $15. Vendors moved steadily up and down the lines selling cakes, pies, newspapers. Others did a profitable business carrying cans of coffee to persons in the line.

Because of the lack of women and an established home life, the saloons of early San Francisco were the social centers of the city. Supplied with newspapers and periodicals, they served as the San Franciscan's club. Open from morning to late at night, much business was carried on in saloons. The larger ones had bands of musicians, whose playing attracted people to their establishments. Every kind of card and gambling game imaginable was offered to the public, and every type and brand of drink was available.

Many forty-niners on their way home, or while passing through the city, would enter these gaudy establishments. Tempted by the chance to double their money, they would try their luck.

As soon as a new-comer has reached the gaming-table fresh from the diggings, he unbuckles his girdle of yellow leather, and gives it a slight shake, placing one of the ends of it on the green tapis. Several pieces of gold roll forth on the table. The head-manager stretches out his large and bony hand, seizes and weighs them in a balance placed at his side, and then declares their value in ounces of eighty-five francs each. The play begins; the same bony hand lifts the piece; the play is resumed to the same result. At the end of 15 or 20 minutes, the girdle must be unloosed once more. It rarely happens that the fool with-

draws before the bank has spoiled him in one night of the fruit of several months' toil and privation.

As the city expanded and more gambling houses and saloons were opened, the demand for female companionship grew. Responsive to the law of supply and demand, women came flocking in to the city in larger numbers. Adventuresses, prostitutes, monte and faro dealers, waitresses, laundresses, and cooks found their place in the hustle and bustle of this mushrooming town.

Gambling houses employed women as a lure for the customers. They worked as bartenders and card dealers to entice men inside and to persuade them to drink and to bet. Many Mexican and Chilean women sold themselves as indentured servants to pay their passage money to California, only to find themselves trapped in houses of prostitution, in order to work out their travel cost. Numerous prostitutes and their pimps and protectors came from France. By 1853, there were more than forty-five houses of prostitution in San Francisco, most of them flourishing.

Many women came as actresses and performers in theater troupes, circuses, concert and dance groups. The few "respectable" women in California had also to work hard to earn their living. They were employed in running boardinghouses, cooking, and laundering, and the demand for their services was so great they could make a good living by their labor.

Mary Ballou and her husband left their sons behind in New Hampshire and came out to California in 1851 to work at a boardinghouse. Describing her work, Mary Ballou wrote:

A ship's cabin turned into a shore restaurant

Sometimes I am washing and ironing, sometimes I am making mince, apple and squash pie. I make biscuits and now and then Indian Johnny cake and then again I am making Indian pudding. Sometimes I am making gruel for the sick, now and then cooking oysters, sometimes making coffee for the French people strong enough for any man to walk on. Three times a day I set my table which is about thirty feet in length and do all the little fixings about it, such as filling pepper boxes and vinegar cruets. . . . Sometimes I am taking care of babies and nursing at the rate of fifty dollars a week, but I would not advise any lady to come out here and suffer the toil and fatigue that I have suffered for the sake of a little gold.

Writing far into the night, Mrs. Ballou told of the bitter cold as winter approached: "It is quite cold here. My fingers are so cold that I can hardly hold my pen. Well, it is ten o'clock at night while I am writing. There, I hear the hogs in my kitchen, turning the pots and kettles upside down. So I must drop my pen and run and drive them out." Sadly, she closed her letter by telling Selden, her oldest boy, "to see that Augustus has every thing that he needs" and to have him warmly dressed: "I worry a great deal about my Dear children. It seems as though my heart would break when I realize how far I am from my Dear loved ones. Thus from your affectionate mother, Mary B. Ballou."

The Miner's Dream

The min- er when he goes to sleep, soon be-gins to snore; Dreams a-bout his friends at home whom he may see no more. A love - ly wife, a sis - ter dear he

may have left be - hind; Per -

haps a fath - er old and gray, a

moth - er good and kind. Now will you, say will you,

lis - ten while I sing A

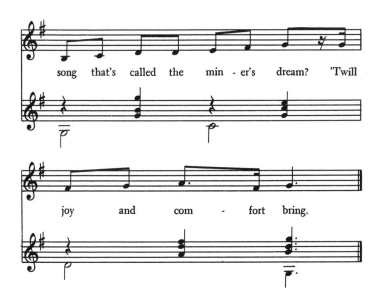

song that's called the min - er's dream? 'Twill

joy and com - fort bring.

The miner when he goes to sleep, soon begins to snore;
Dreams about his friends at home whom he may see no more.
A lovely wife, a sister dear he may have left behind;
Perhaps a father old and gray, a mother good and kind.

CHORUS:
Now will you, say will you, listen while I sing
A song that's called the miner's dream?
'Twill joy and comfort bring.

His boyhood years return again, his heart is filled with joy—
Is rolling hoops or playing ball as when he was a boy.
'Tis winter time—he's skating now, of which he was so fond;
'Tis summer now—he's swimming in the old familiar pond!

CHORUS

His boyhood days are past and gone, for now he is a man—
Is going to California to try the pick and pan;
Bright visions now of happiness are dancing o'er his mind;
Disturb him not, but let him dream so long as he's inclined.

CHORUS

His mind is home among the fields of wheat and yellow corn—
Sits down beneath an apple tree, all shady in the morn—
But morning comes—and at his door a neighbor gently knocks;
He wakes, and finds himself in bed among the hills and rocks.

CHORUS

PRIDE AND PREJUDICE

When the miners began to flock to the gold fields in 1848, California was still a territory; it was ruled by the military government that had been established there during the Mexican War. Then, in 1850, this territory was admitted to the Union as a state.

The forty-niners regarded the gold strikes as made on public land owned by the federal government. Here was land not owned by any private individual; all Americans —at least those white and native born—had access to and the right to use it. Here was land free of established government, which the people could democratically organize and rule. Here was land where the working miner could move in, be his own boss, work hard, and get rich.

How did it work out? To a great extent the miners did devise their own mining laws and regulations—in a spirit and tradition of American self-government that ran all the way back to the Mayflower Compact.

The miners put all men for once upon a level. Clothes, money, manners, family connections, letters of introduction, never before counted for so little. The whole community was substantially given an equal start in the race. . . . Each stranger was welcomed, told to take pick and pan and go to work for himself. The richest miner in the camp was seldom able to hire a servant; those who had formerly been glad to serve others, were digging in their own claims.

So wrote Charles Shinn in his classic *Mining Camps: A Study in American Frontier Government.*

In almost every camp a mass meeting of all the miners was held to elect a committee to draw up a set of mining laws that would regulate their daily life. A man was allowed to claim a reasonable square footage of land on which to mine, varying in size from ten to thirty square feet. The richer the diggings, the smaller the claim. Its size was always regulated by the limits of what a man could actually work. He was not allowed to hold his claim or speculate on it or rent it to others. Only one claim at a time could be held by each miner. His title was not absolute; he did not own the land, but merely had the right to use it for mining purposes.

In most camps a miner had to work his claim at least once a week; if he did not, he lost it, and anyone else could take it over. Usually the claim had to be marked and boundaries staked. One miner put up a sign notifying others of his property rights in no uncertain terms:

NOTIS: *To all and everybody. This is my claim, fifty feet on the gulch, cordin' to Clear Creek District Law, backed up by shotgun ammendments.—Thomas Hall*

Many disagreements arose about who had the right to work the land. In almost all cases, if the two parties could not settle it themselves, a miners' meeting was called. All who swung a pick or held a claim were eligible to be chosen to sit on the jury. The following song describes such a meeting.

The Miners' Meeting

When miners get into a row about their mining claims
A miners' meeting then is called, and miners flock around;
Each party clearly states his case, then both proclaim aloud,
"We'll introduce our evidence, then leave it to the crowd."

A witness then is called upon, who tells a crooked yarn,
Declares the diggings "jumpable" as as far as he can "larn,"
Is positive they've not been worked as mining law requires,
And any man that says they have, he'll tell him *he's a liar*.

A witness on the other side tells quite another tale,
An interested party then presents a bill of sale,
And proves it clear and furthermore that he's been very sick,
Not able since he bought the claim to strike a single lick.

Now "Bob" brings up a man and proves "he has not been unwell,
But since the date of bill of sale has been as drunk as h-ll."
The friends of "Bob" begin to howl and "Jake's" begin to swear,
A few go in and fight it out or "try it on the square."

A call is made from either side to hear the ayes and noes—
By this time half the crowd is drunk, and care not how it goes;
And all begin to curse and swear, and out with bowie knives,
All ready, should it come to blows, to take each other's lives.

A drunken bully in the crowd throws off his hat and coat,
And right or wrong, no matter which, he thus demands the vote—
"Now all in favor of old Bob, will please to holler, 'AYE'
And all who vote the other way shall leave the diggings dry."

The crowd sends forth a hideous howl, and Bob has won the day,
Who now invites all hands to drink before they go away.
Old Jake concludes he's badly beat, and quietly retires,
Well satisfied that Bob has raised *the largest crowd of liars!*

The jury would call witnesses, hear evidence from both parties, and then render its verdict. "Very near where we were at work," wrote Borthwick,

a party of half-a-dozen men held a claim in the bed of the creek, and had as usual dug a race through which to turn the water, and so leave exposed the part they intended to work. They were opposed by a number of miners whose claims lay so near the race that they would have been swamped had the water been turned into it.

Unable to settle the dispute among themselves, they sent a notice to all the miners within two or three miles up and down the creek. About a hundred miners presented themselves, and the two opposing sides chose six jurors each. With the rest of the miners sitting around, smoking their pipes, the jury listened to both sides.

They then called some more witnesses to give further information, and having laid their shaggy heads together for a few minutes, they pronounced their decision: which was, that the men working on the race should be allowed six days to work out their claims before the water should be turned in upon them.

Neither party was particularly well pleased with the verdict—a pretty good sign that it was an impartial one; but they had to abide by it, for had there been any resistance on either side, the rest of the miners would have enforced the decision.

In the early days of 1848 and the beginnings of 1849, miners seemed to be quite honest, and there was almost no crime in the diggings. A man's word was his bond. Wash basins, jars, and sacks of gold dust could be left unguarded in tents and cabins while miners were away working their claims. Tools and supplies were left lying around, and there was little stealing or jumping of claims.

As time went on, crime and dishonesty increased in the mines. Upon the discovery of a crime and the apprehension of a culprit, a miners' meeting would be called. The case was heard, and a judgment was rendered. As there were no jails or prisons in which to confine the criminals, the verdict was swiftly carried out. Punishment usually consisted of whipping, banishment, or hanging. Whipping was a common penalty for crimes of theft.

As far as most of the miners were concerned, mining law and enforcement worked. Yet there were many abuses. Passions often ran high; excitement and violence ruled the day, and mob law prevailed.

"A scene occurred about this time," wrote Buffum in January 1849, "that exhibits in a striking light, the summary manner in which 'justice' is dispensed of in a community where there are no legal tribunes." Five men had been arrested for armed robbery. They received thirty-nine lashes each. Then, fresh charges of robbery and attempted murder during the previous fall were preferred against three of them, two Frenchmen and a Chilean. Too weak from the beating to attend their own trial, the proceedings went on without them.

They were tried in the open air by a crowd of some two hundred men who had organized themselves into a jury, and appointed a pro tempore judge. The charges against them were nothing more than an attempt at robbery and murder. They were known to be bad men, however, and a general sentiment seemed to prevail in the crowd that they ought to be got rid of.

Judge Brown holds court

The trial lasted thirty minutes. The judge asked the crowd whether they were guilty or not. The answer was a thunderous "Yes!" When the judge asked the crowd what punishment should be inflicted, someone shouted, "Hang them!" The angry miners proceeded to carry out the execution. Ropes were put around the prisoners' necks, and they were placed on a wagon.

No time was given them for explanation. They vainly tried to speak, but none of them understood English. Vainly they called for an interpreter, but their cries were drowned by the yells of the now infuriated mob. A black handkerchief was bound around the eyes of each; their arms were pinioned and at a given signal, without priest or prayerbook, the wagon was drawn from under them and they were launched into eternity.

Much of the crime, cruelty, and discrimination found in the mines was practiced against foreigners. While the forty-niners firmly believed that every man had an equal right to his fair share of gold, this right extended only to white, native-born Americans. The great majority of the forty-niners were Protestants, and their ethnic background was mainly English. They had an inborn contempt for Spanish, Mexican, and South American people.

The forty-niners also brought with them and put into practice the frontier tradition of squatting on free public land. In the peace treaty signed with Mexico, the United States had pledged that the property and other rights of the Mexican settlers would be honored and respected. The flood of forty-niners paid little attention to such promises or to the property rights of the Californian Mexicans.

The Mexican settlers frequently took their claims to court, but their cases dragged on for years. Even if they won their cases, it did not help much. Squatters overran their land and could not be driven off.

Not all the Anglos were prejudiced against other American people. T. T. Johnson remembers how a spirit of brotherhood and comradeship existed in the early mining camps:

Pitching our tents on the borders of the American River, we found ourselves surrounded by Peruvians, Chileans, Mexicans, Kanakas, and our own countrymen, as well as Europeans of every kind, class and description. . . . Convicts whose term had expired in Botany Bay, educated Americans and Europeans, or Kanakas, fresh from Honolulu, were all on an equal footing.

Many Mexicans, Chileans, Colombians, and other Central and South Americans were experienced and knowledgeable miners. They brought a great deal of skill and technique to the mining camps which proved invaluable to the inexperienced Anglos. When the forty-niners first arrived, they were, wrote Kelley, quick to ask advice from the Spanish-speaking miners: But, "as soon as Jonathan got an inkling of the system, with peculiarly bad taste and ungenerous feelings, he organized a crusade against these obliging strangers and ran them off the creek at pistol mouth."

A great number of forty-niners were veterans of the Mexican War, and hostile feelings were still left over from that conflict. "The Spanish-Americans are held in sovereign contempt by citizens," wrote Pringle Shaw, a forty-niner, "and are stigmatized with being filthy, ignorant, lazy and vicious":

South Americans winnowing gold

In truth, it must be owned that the poor Spaniards have been more sinned against than sinning. Hundreds have been murdered and ruthlessly driven from their homes for acts of depredation committed by Americans. No sooner is a crime committed, than suspicion falls immediately on some unfortunate Mexican or Chileno. The accusers are by no means expected to prove the victim guilty, but he is commanded to prove his innocence. They have in many cases suffered more persecutions, even, than the Chinese.

Numbers of mining camps passed codes excluding foreigners from the diggings. In 1852, the state legislature enacted the first anti-foreign legislation in Cailfornia's history. The Foreign Miners' License Law imposed a special tax of $20 per month on miners who were not citizens of the United States. Restrictive laws, threats, and actual violence drove thousands of Mexicans, Chileans, Peruvians, and Colombians out of California.

Soon Anglo prejudice focused on the Chinese miners. By 1852, 25,000 Chinese had emigrated to the "Golden Mountains," their name for California. Many young men, with dreams like those of the American gold-seekers, were going to strike it rich, make their fortunes, and return to their families in China. Many failed to find gold and could not pay the high price of return passage to China. They worked in San Francisco and other towns as servants, waiters, launderers, laborers, and businessmen; and they were much in demand. Kelley wrote:

There are a great number of Chinese in California, most of whom settle in the cities, partially adopting the prevailing costume, a very useful class of men, quick, industrious and persevering; they are systematic, sober and cleanly, and when treated with proper kindness and indulgence, become attached and interested. They, above all others, appear successful in finding employment; for you never see a Chinese lolling about, or amongst the group of idlers. They soon become possessed of means from the simplicity of their habits and economy of their domestic menage [household] and do not hesitate to share it in establishing their countrymen.

As long as the miners prospered and jobs were plentiful, the Chinese were tolerated. However, more and more Chinese became miners at the same time as the opportunities for individual miners to acquire a quick fortune faded. Gold mining was in the process of becoming a big business, employing low-paid laborers and absentee capital. Many of the Chinese miners would work for such low wages and were so industrious that the mining companies hired them rather than the Americans. Many individual forty-niners, unable to make a living in the mines, flocked to the towns and cities to take other jobs and found the Chinese holding many of them. Racial feelings intensified, and the persecution of the Chinese increased.

To the eyes and ears of the North Americans, the language, appearance, and customs of the Chinese seemed to be so foreign as to make them subhuman. There was little thought that they were individuals far from home, away from their loved ones, suffering loneliness and discouragement, experiencing hardship and privation as much as any American forty-niner.

A song found in several California songbooks of the 1850s ridiculed "John Chinaman" and took him to task for not being trustworthy and for not Americanizing

Chinese mining camp

himself. The song repeated many of the prejudices and narrow-minded biases against the Chinese and criticized them as interested only in finding gold. As though any pure-blooded American forty-niner was truly interested in anything else!

Laws were passed by the State of California directed against the Chinese, barring them from citizenship, forbidding them from owning or buying real estate, and denying them licenses to open businesses. After the Civil War, Chinese children, along with Indian and Black children, were forbidden to attend public schools.

Another group discriminated against were Blacks. From the earliest days of Spanish settlement, Blacks had played a role in California. They were among the earliest settlers of Los Angeles. By 1852, there were over two thousand Blacks in California. Some were free Blacks, others were brought into the area as slaves by their masters. Many were miners who worked in the diggings side by side with other miners. Other Blacks settled in San Francisco and Sacramento and worked as cooks, waiters, stewards, porters, barbers, mechanics, and businessmen.

The Constitutional Convention that met at Monterey in September 1849 drew up a state constitution. By a unanimous vote, it outlawed slavery in California. When Congress admitted California as a state in 1850, she entered as a free state.

The action against slavery in California was not as much a humane declaration against the evils of slavery as an economic protest. Many delegates to the convention were miners or representatives of mining districts. The miners felt that they did not want plantation owners coming to the mines with large numbers of their slaves who would work in the diggings for them and, by their labor, monopolize the gold. Free miners could not, they believed, compete against such competition. Also, many of them felt that the hard, physical work all miners did should not be demeaned by allowing slaves to work the mines, too, as this would reflect on all miners.

Blacks had few rights and were discriminated against by acts of the state legislature. They were not allowed to vote or to testify in court cases involving whites until 1863, when the Republican party became a powerful force in the State.

From its inception, then, California has had a long history of racial legislation, which has been supported by majorities of her voters. Much of it has been struck down by the courts. But, as much as the Mexicans, South Americans, Chinese, and Blacks suffered, the worst discrimination was shown to the original settlers, the California Indians. They were to be hunted down, driven off, murdered, and finally wiped out.

John Chinaman

John — Chin - a - man, John Chin - a - man, But —

five short years a - go, I — wel - comed you from

Can - ton, John, But I wish I had - n't

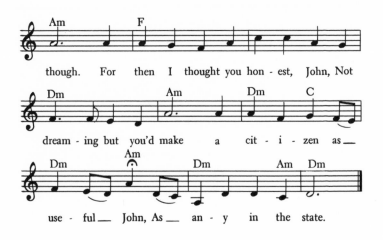

though. For then I thought you hon-est, John, Not dream-ing but you'd make a cit-i-zen as— use-ful— John, As— an-y in the state.

John Chinaman, John Chinaman
    But five short years ago,
I welcomed you from Canton, John—
    But I wish I hadn't though.
For then I thought you honest, John,
    Not dreaming but you'd make
A citizen as useful, John,
    As any in the State.

I thought you'd open wide your ports,
    And let our merchants in,
To barter for their crapes and teas,
    Their wares of wood and tin.
I thought you'd cut your queue off, John,
    And don a Yankee coat,
And a collar high you'd raise, John,
    Around your dusty throat.

I imagined that the truth, John,
    You'd speak when under oath,
But I find you'll lie and steal too—
    Yes, John, you're up to both.
I thought of rats and puppies, John,
    You'd eaten your last fill,
But on such slimy pot-pies, John,
    I'm told you dinner still.

Oh, John, I've been deceived in you,
    And in all your thieving clan,
For our gold is all you're after, John,
    To get it as you can.
John Chinaman, John Chinaman
    But five short years ago,
I welcomed you from Canton, John—
    But I wish I hadn't though.

THE EXTERMINATION OF
THE CALIFORNIA INDIANS

The California Indians suffered most from the gold rush simply because they were there. Their lands were either in the diggings or on the roads to them. The forty-niners had little understanding or respect for the Indian culture and way of life. Wherever and whenever Indians were in the way, the Americans simply swept them aside. Caught up in a drive for riches, the white men were in no mood to tolerate any opposition or to worry about whose lands they were on, whose streams they were fouling, whose burial grounds they were defiling. No treacherous, ignorant savage (said they) was going to stand in the way of their pursuit of the rainbow. White men's disease, white men's greed, white men's alcohol destroyed the Indian peoples.

The Indians lived in the interior valleys and deserts in an area largely untouched by the advance of Spanish civilization. But it was into this interior that the flood of Anglo-Americans was now moving. Prospectors penetrated and explored every canyon, valley, and gulch in search for gold. Wherever a strike or discovery was made, forty-niners poured in, and mining camps sprang up. Within a year, the Anglos outnumbered the Indians.

The Indians watched with dismay the invasion of their territory, the slaughter of their game, and the poisoning and polluting of their streams by mining sludge and refuse. Many of the acorn-producing oaks and nut-bearing pines were chopped down and the timber used to build cabins, dams, and sluices.

In 1855, Phillip H. Sheridan, then an army lieutenant serving in California, reported coming across a band of Pit River Indians.

Indians are always hungry, but these poor creatures were particularly so, as their usual supply of food had grown very scarce. In former years salmon were very abundant in the streams of the Sacramento Valley, and every fall they took great quantities of these fish and dried them for winter use, but alluvial mining has of late years defiled the water of the different streams and driven the fish out. On this account the usual supply of salmon was very limited. They got some trout high up on the rivers, above the sluices and rockers of the miners, but this was a precarious source from which to derive food.

In the mining towns and the diggings themselves, the Indians were held in lowest esteem and treated with contempt. In 1848 they were allowed to mine either for themselves or as laborers for white bosses. But as the mines filled up with forty-niners arriving from the East and Oregon, the Indians were ordered off the land and driven out. The impact on the Indians of this sudden contact with the civilization of the mining camps quickly produced deadly effects on the culture of the peaceful and unsuspecting natives.

Grimshaw, one of the early prospectors in 1848, who later on became a storekeeper, tells how the Indians from the Sierra foothills were first lured to the mines by the Mexican rancheros.

When the gold was discovered, many of the rancheros hastened to the foothills with droves of cattle, and in course of time, supplies of flour, hard bread, sugar, raisins, beads, dry goods and clothing; spiritous liquors being by common consent rigidly taboo. The Indians worked with great energy to acquire the heretofore unheard of luxuries supplied by the traders. . . .

As newcomers made their appearance and competition in trade commenced, the Indians were freely supplied with liquor by the newly-established white traders and of course, became greatly demoralized. Their early protectors, the rancheros, left the mines in disgust; the poor aborigines were abandoned to the mercy of a number of semi-barbarous white men, and died and were killed off with frightful rapidity.

The Indian culture began to change. What were luxuries and novelties at first, began to take on importance and become necessities. Emulating the white man's dress and style of living, lured by the possibility of possessing things they had never owned or desired before, the Indians became enmeshed in the digging of gold to satisfy these new desires. They abandoned their ancestral way of life and fell victim to artificial longings. An article in the New York *Herald* of December 3, 1848, reported:

The Indians constitute the principal part of the laborers, and their condition is entirely changed. Instead of being content, as formerly, with only a breechclout, they seek fine clothes and pay enormous prices for them.

Large quantities of goods were daily sent forward to

the mines, as the Indians heretofore poor and depraved, have suddenly become consumers of the luxuries of life.

Hubert Bancroft, the historian, from his vantage point in California, gives us this more detailed view of the Indian as a consumer:

The Mexican serape was quite becoming to the California root digger and took his fancy wonderfully. In the absence of a serape, however, an American blanket would do, and for this, of a quality worth $4 or $5, they cheerfully paid Weber, the Coloma shopkeeper, $100. Before the end of 1848, thousands of savages, who up to that time had lived on roots and acorns, and had paraded the forests as naked as Adam in the garden, were arrayed in gorgeous apparel costing $500, conspicuous in which was gaudy calico, red handkerchiefs, hat, shirt, pantaloons and blanket or serape. For food in place of acorns and mashed grasshoppers, they purchased almonds and raisins at $16 a pound; and for a bottle of whiskey, they paid $16.

Because their culture did not stress accumulation and greed, the Indians were scarcely a match for the shrewd white storekeeper or prospector, who often cheated and shortchanged them. Relates Grimshaw: "In trading with Indians, it was considered legitimate (even in the stores at Sutter's Fort) to have two sets of weights. The Indian ounce weight was equal to two ounces standard and so on up."

As the number of gold-seekers increased and the search for gold intensified, the whites were less and less inclined to allow the Indians to prospect in the diggings. Many Oregonians emigrated to the gold fields, and they arrived utterly prejudiced in their feelings about the Indians.

States Grimshaw: "Instances were by no means rare where an Indian, working a piece of ground and hesitating about giving it up at the command of some white ruffian [was] ruthlessly shot down and his body tossed aside to be burned or buried by the members of his tribe."

While whites often escaped without punishment for such crimes, the sins of the red men were much more seriously dealt with. John Doble casually noted in his diary an example of the justice meted out to both Indian and white man.

An Indian was shot for stealing by some emigrants up the road 9 or 10 miles yesterday which has created a little stir among the Indians, but not of any consequence. An emigrant was taken up today for trying to sell a horse he had picked up near here which belonged to a man in this town. He was let off with a fine.

Whites often jumped to hasty and unjustified conclusions about the guilt of the red men whenever a theft occurred. Delano states:

It had become common to charge every theft of cattle on the Indians. A party of miners missed several head of oxen, and a cry was raised that the Indians had stolen them. Fifteen men were started out, well armed, swearing vengeance. Proceeding to a rancheria, they found a few bones, which they considered proof positive of the guilt of the inhabitants. They immediately surrounded the huts and when the Indians came out, a deadly discharge of firearms was made and fourteen Indians fell dead. After demolishing the houses, the brave whites set out on their return. When they had nearly reached home, their sense of justice was a little shaken, by seeing every ox which they had supposed stolen, quietly feeding in a somewhat isolated gorge, whither they had strayed in search of grass. Had the Indians, under similar circumstances, killed fourteen whites, an exterminating warfare would have ensued.

This brutality was widespread in the mines. To many whites, killing an Indian was the same as shooting a wild animal. Cruel jokes were also played on the red men. Such barbarism helped to relieve the monotony of mining life. Bancroft relates one such "humorous" incident:

One Sunday in August, 1850, in the town of Sonoma a person called Cave in conversation with a gambler named Mason, pointing to an Indian who was lounging about the street, offered to lay a wager that he could induce the native to rob or kill him (Mason). Mason accepted the offer. Cave then drew the native aside; told him that Mason had a large sum of money hidden; told him where he should find it and that if he would rob or kill Mason, he should have half of it and no harm should befall him. Placing an unloaded pistol in his hand, Cave urged him on to the consummation of the deed. Irresolute, bewildered, worked upon more by the exhortations of Cave than any desire to do wrong, the native hesitantly entered Mason's house, looked around and came out without touching a thing. Mason was watching for him and as soon as he was fairly on the street again, shot him dead. No one was punished for this incident.

Sometimes the Indians fought back. If they could not find the white man who had committed the crime, they avenged the wrong upon the first whites they met. Thus innocent people on both sides were often caught in the middle, and suffered. From 1849 through 1852, open warfare broke out in many places throughout the state. The land ran red with blood and killings.

California's first governor was Peter H. Burnett from Oregon. Burnett, in his annual message of 1851 to the California Legislature stated his belief that "a war of extermination will continue to be waged between the races until the Indian race becomes extinct. . . . While we cannot anticipate the result but with painful regret, the inevitable destiny of the race is beyond the power of men to avert."

Outnumbering the Indians, with superior weapons, usually without any burden of women and children to defend, the whites were more mobile and aggressive. They organized posses and local militia and struck back against any Indians they could find. They burned down whole villages, whether the people in them were innocent or not of any wrongdoing. The Indians fought back as best they could, but it was a hopeless struggle against impossible odds. When they stood and fought, they were killed. Their only alternative was to surrender and be run out of their ancestral homeland, to end up on reservations as prisoners of the federal government.

The California legislature appropriated half a million dollars to be used to "settle" the Indian problem. Many forty-niners found that by joining the state militia they would be provided with high pay and bed and board and could do much better financially than by continuing to dig for gold.

Coupled, then, with vengeance and racial hatred was greed. Many whites made a good living out of warring against the Indians, either as volunteer militia or as suppliers of the military campaigns. When an expedition was fitted out against the red men, claims were filed with state and local officials for payment for salaries, supplies, horses, arms and ammunition. The state politicians passed these costs along to the federal government. In the 1850s California was reimbursed more than $2 million by the U.S. government, a huge sum for that time, in monies that the state claimed it had spent in the fighting against the Indians. The chance for pay and profits in warring against the Indians may have done much to drag out the hostilities.

After the secularization of the missions in 1834–36, the Indian population in Los Angeles had increased. Many Indians from the surrounding areas came to the city looking for work. The Mexicans had perpetuated an old Spanish custom in Los Angeles of arresting drunken Indians and putting them on work gangs to maintain and repair the main-water ditch which carried water to the town.

Often, there were too many Indians to be thus employed, and the jails were filled to overflowing. Feeding and housing the prisoners was expensive. To rectify this, the City Council with American efficiency in August 1850 added a refinement that would make sure no Indian would escape work and would also raise funds for the city. They passed two resolutions. The first ordinance stated that "the city's prisoners shall be formed in a chain gang and occupied in public work." The second proclaimed:

When the city has no work in which to employ the chain gang, the Recorder shall, by means of notices con-

spicuously posted, notify the public that such a number of prisoners will be auctioned off to the highest bidder for private service and in that manner they shall be disposed of for a sum which shall not be less than the amount of their fines for double the time they were to serve in hard labor.

Thus, on Sundays at sundown, the town police would round up all the Indians found in the streets. They were usually workers—men, women, and children—from the local vineyards, who had been paid off on Saturday, usually in aguardiente, a powerful native liquor. The workers would spend Saturday night and Sunday drinking, gambling, and socializing, trying to relax from the heavy labor they had done. W. W. Robinson, who wrote a small but powerful and descriptive book on *The Indians of Los Angeles: The Story of the Liquidation of a People*, tells us what happened next:

Arrested, they were driven or dragged to a nearby corral, . . . to sleep off their liquor. Monday morning they were put up for sale, for one week, to the highest bidders. Vineyards and others wanting workers were on hand. Prices paid averaged one dollar to three dollars per Indian. One third of this sum went to the Indian at the end of the week—in the form of aguardiente—two-thirds, in money to the city of Los Angeles. The next weekend was spent again in debauchery with the victims up at the Monday morning slave market. This process was repeated weekly. The effect on the individual Indian was to destroy him in one, two or three years.

In the north also, the Indians were regarded as a cheap

supply of labor. Employed by landowners at whatever rates they chose to pay them, the red men were treated in some cases worse than slaves. Indeed, there was a widespread and continuing practice of kidnapping Indian children to be sold into perpetual slavery as household and farm servants. Speaking about the treatment of Indians in the northern part of the state, J. Ross Browne, federal inspector of Indian affairs, commented:

The settlers engaged them at a fixed rate of wages to cultivate the ground, and during the season of labor fed them on beans, and gave them a blanket or shirt each; after which, when the harvest was secured, the account was considered squared, and the Indian was driven off to forage in the woods for themselves and families during the winter. . . . Of those that failed to perish from hunger or exposure, some were killed on the general principle that they must have subsisted by stealing cattle, for it was well known that cattle ranged in the vicinity, while others were not unfrequently slaughtered by their employers for helping themselves to the refuse portions of the crop which had been left in the ground.

By 1851, officially appointed Indian commissioners from Washington arrived in California. They went into the countryside to make contact with the Indians. By March 1851, the Maidu, a tribe of mountain Indians who were the first Indians the commissioners treated with, were compelled to sign treaties giving up all claim to their territory and transferring the remnants of their tribe to so-called reservations. Describing these reservations, Kroeber, one of the leading authorities on California Indians and an anthropologist, says:

The first reservations established by Federal officers in California were little else than bull pens. They were founded on the principle, not of attempting to do something for the native, but of getting him out of the white man's way as cheaply and hurriedly as possible.

Other treaties were made with 123 tribes in other sections of the state. The commissioners were often fairminded men who tried to treat the Indians as people with rights. Nevertheless, the treaties were unsatisfactory to the people and legislature of California. Much of the land set aside for the reservations was in rich agricultural and mining areas. It was impractical to think that the white settlers would allow it to be permanently inhabited by Indians. Bitterly opposed by both of California's United States senators, the treaties were ultimately rejected by the Senate.

The desperate Indians resorted to warfare. In 1853 a new series of treaties were made with them, and smaller reservations were set up on less desirable land. Here they would be protected from molestation by the whites by companies of the U.S. Army. However, these reservations were subject to abuse and corruption by the Indian agents appointed to supervise them. The spoils system predominated; every time a new administrator was chosen for the Indian Department, he brought in new personnel and agents who were his friends or to whom he owed favors. Most of the agents were more interested in lining their own pockets than in carefully and wisely dispersing the sums appropriated by Congress for the welfare of the Indians.

J. Ross Browne, an Irish immigrant, was appointed in 1855 Customs Official and Inspector of Indian Affairs.

Fearless and honest, he raged against the corruption of the agents and commented, "An honest Indian agent is the rarest work of God I know."

Congress appropriated large sums of money for the purchase of cattle and agricultural implements for the Indians. Commissioners were appointed at handsome salaries. Wrote Browne:

> Treaties were made in which the various tribes were promised a great many valuable presents, which of course, they never got. There was no reason to suppose they ever should; it being a fixed principle with strong powers never to ratify treaties made by their own agents with weaker ones, when there is money to pay and nothing to be had in return.

Often the cattle were driven up to the mines and slaughtered and sold to the miners at exorbitant rates. The money was pocketed by the agents entrusted with the cattle. Clothing and blankets given to the Indians were of the cheapest and coarsest quality, while the prices charged back to Congress were of the highest. Again the agents received their share of the profits from the dishonest suppliers and manufacturers.

The agents were also able to make money from supervising the health care and physical needs of the Indians. Since the agents were the ones who appointed and supervised the doctors who worked on the reservations, corruption flourished here as well. The sufferings and illnesses of the Indians were a constant source of profits to both agent and doctor.

The Indians continued to resist abuse by the whites. The final battle in California took place in 1873 in the

Modoc War, a war that caught the attention of the world. The Indian chief, Captain Jack, with 50 fighting men and 150 women and children, led his group away from the reservation they were forced to share with a tribe of traditional enemies. They wanted to return to their ancestral home, a land of little value to the whites. The government would not permit them to do so. They must move back to the reservation set aside for them— peacefully if possible, forcibly if necessary.

Though they fought gallantly and at first with some success, the Indians were overwhelmed and worn down by army units armed with howitzers, Indian allies, and superior forces. The war lasted three months; it ended in the court-martial and execution of Captain Jack and three of his men, and the removal of the remnants of his band back to the reservation. This "war" cost the U.S. government 83 dead and over a million dollars; but the Indians had been taught who was master.

On the morning of August 29, 1911, sleeping butchers in a slaughterhouse near Oroville, California, were awakened by the barking of their dogs. They saw a man, an Indian, crouching against the fence. Almost naked, his hair burned down close to his scalp, he was thin, emaciated. Fearful, unable to speak a word of English, the Indian was gently taken to the Oroville jail until the sheriff could find out what to do with him.

The story of the "wild man" made the newspapers. Two anthropologists, Professors Kroeber and Waterman of the University of California, were extremely interested. Waterman came down to the jail to visit the Indian. He soon succeeded in establishing that he was a descendant of the extinct tribe of the Yahi Indians. Waterman named him Ishi, meaning "man" in the Yahi language.

Ishi was the last wild Indian in North America, a man who had lived most of his life in the Stone Age culture. Taken by Waterman to San Francisco, Ishi was to live for four and a half years at the university's Museum of Anthropology. In those brief years he entered the twentieth century and contributed a tremendous amount of knowledge to anthropologists about the culture of the Yahi. Ishi gave insight into their way of life and explained how he had managed to be the last survivor of his people.

The Yahi, numbering two to three thousand souls, were reduced to less than fifty individuals in their struggle to preserve their lands against the white settlers. As a small boy of three or four, Ishi experienced an attack on his village at Mill Creek by the local volunteer militia led by Robert A. Anderson, a scout and tracker. Attacking in the quiet dawn of August 16, 1865, the militia mercilessly shot down the Indians. Anderson reported that "many dead bodies floated down the rapid current." The village was ransacked and burned; the dead were stripped of their scalps, which the white men proudly wore as decorations on their clothing.

Ishi, his mother, and a few other Yahi Indians escaped. From that time on, Ishi and his companions hid in terror from any whites. These were the years called "the Long Concealment." Remaining in the hills among the volcanic rocks, sheltering in the gorges and caves, living precariously off the land, the small group preserved their freedom, refusing to surrender to the white men. Wild as any creatures of the earth, sharing their land with the deer, bear, and snake, they survived only to die one by one of old age, hardship, starvation, and exposure.

By 1908, only four Yahi were left: Ishi, his mother, his sister, and an old man. In November of that year, an engineering party of the Oro Light and Power Company which was building a dam in the vicinity came across their encampment. Ishi's sister and the old man fled, never to be seen again. Ishi helped his old and sick mother to get away. Soon after this she died, leaving Ishi completely alone. For over three years he lived without human companionship, until he emerged from the woods in August 1911, starved and exhausted.

Ishi's story is beautifully and movingly told by Theodora Kroeber in her book *Ishi: In Two Worlds*. As Ishi walked with Professor Waterman from the jail to the station where the train was to take them to San Francisco, he was filled with many thoughts. Ishi must have seen the train, the white man's demon, hundreds of times when he was hiding in the chaparral and wilderness of Mill Creek and Deer Creek. His mother had assured him that it would not hurt any Indian.

Today, Ishi wondered. He had not been so near it before; it was larger, and noisier and speedier than he had realized. Would the Demon know that he was Indian? He was wearing white men's clothes, and his hair was short like theirs. It might be as well to watch from a little distance, from the shelter of a tree or bush, as he was accustomed to, at least until he made sure that his friend was correct in his assurance that the Demon always stayed in its own old tracks, and that it carried people safely from place to place. The white men who

Ishi: a photograph published in 1914

should have the most reason to be afraid, showed no signs of uneasiness, rather they climbed in and out of it, and one of them sat in its head waving to those below. Ishi came back onto the platform, and made no objection to going aboard with Waterman. He had committed himself too far to turn back now, nor did he wish to do so; where his new friend led he would follow.

Arriving in San Francisco, Ishi lived at the museum. He became famous. He willingly demonstrated for the public who crowded to see him the ancient Yahi arts of bow making, arrow fashioning, and making fire with the fire-bow. He was dignified, reserved but friendly, calmly accepting the interest in himself and his crafts.

Waterman and Kroeber, along with Saxon Pope, the doctor from the university hospital, became Ishi's close friends and guardians, protecting him from the showmen and humbugs who wanted to exploit him. These three scientists learned to respect Ishi for his humaneness, his dignity and self-respect, and his knowledge. In a brief period, Ishi, who had lived for five decades in the wilderness, bridged thousands of years of culture. He was able to move through the streets of San Francisco as a self-supporting, responsible, and sensitive human being.

In December 1915 Ishi developed a terrible cough. Treated, he seemed to recover, but in August he was back in the hospital. "Civilization had bestowed upon him the gift of tuberculosis." Nursed by Pope, he fought the disease, never complaining. But in the spring of 1916, on March 25, he died.

Deeply moved, mourning the loss of his friend, Pope wrote:

And so, stoic and unafraid, departed the last wild Indian of America. He closes a chapter in history. He looked upon us as sophisticated children—smart, but not wise. He knew many things, and much that is false. He knew nature, which is always true. His were the qualities of character that last forever. He was kind; he had courage and self-restraint, and though all had been taken from him, there was no bitterness in his heart. His soul was that of a child, his mind that of a philosopher.

In accordance with Yahi tradition and Ishi's wishes, his body was cremated and his ashes buried.

Then he was gone, the long journey from the ancient Yana homeland along Mill and Deer creeks to the Land of the Yana Dead completed, his leavetaking from his friends and their world as quiet as his own preferred and understated phrase of farewell: "YOU STAY, I GO."

The Dying Californian

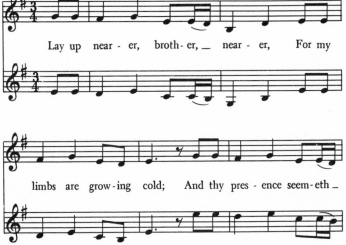

Lay up near-er, broth-er, _ near-er, For my limbs are grow-ing cold; And thy pres-ence seem-eth _

near - er When thine arms a - round me fold. I am

dy - ing, broth - er, dy - ing, Soon you'll miss me in _ your

berth; For my form will soon be _

ly - ing Be-neath the o - cean's brin - y _ surf.

Lay up, nearer, brother, nearer,
     For my limbs are growing cold;
And thy presence seemeth nearer
     When thine arms around me fold.
I am dying, brother, dying,
     Soon you'll miss me in your berth;
For my form will soon be lying
     Beneath the ocean's briny surf.

Tell my father when you see him
     That in death I prayed for him,
Prayed that I might only meet him
     In a world that's free from sin.
Tell my mother, God assist her
     Now that she is growing old,
That her child would glad have kissed her
     When his lips grew pale and cold.

Listen, brother, catch each whisper
     'Tis my wife I speak of now,
Tell, oh tell her how I missed her
     When the fever burned my brow.
Tell her she must kiss my children
     Like the kiss I last impressed,
Hold them as when last I held them
     Held them closely to my breast.

It was for them I crossed the ocean,
     What my hopes were I'll not tell;
But they gained an orphan's portion,
     Yet He doeth all things well;
Tell them I have reached the haven
     Where I sought the precious dust,
But I gained a port called Heaven
     Where the gold will never rust.

ᘰ|10|ᘰ

WEIGHING OUT THE GOLD DUST

From the days of the first settlements in the New World, the prize that always drew the settlers westward was the natural resources of the virgin land. Then, in 1848, gold was found in the Sacramento Valley. As the news spread like wildfire, an electric fever swept the earth.

From every corner of the world, but especially from the eastern and midwestern United States, gold-seekers poured into California. Spanish and Indian customs and culture vanished almost overnight as the Mexican-Americans and Indians were pushed aside by the newcomers.

By ship and by land, the gold-seekers, called forty-niners, made their way to California. Speed was essential. Gold nuggets as big as your fist lay on the ground waiting to be picked up. Whoever got there first would have the best pickings. The cost for passage and equipment was prohibitively high, but who cared? "I'm off to California with my washbowl on my knee."

Persevering through incredible hardships—storms, shipwrecks, bad food, disease, miserable living conditions at sea—ships emptied their human cargo at San Francisco. Those coming overland also suffered on an incredible trip of over two thousand miles, twelve to fifteen miles a day—wagons breaking down, livestock dying, deserts and rivers to cross, cholera, smallpox, accidents as constant companions.

The gold-seekers were representatives of the society from which they came—a materialistic society that was ready to sacrifice everything in life, including life itself, for gold. But there was a positive side to the gold rush. California's gold poured in a steady stream to the federal government and played a large role in helping to preserve the Union during the Civil War. California miners were pioneers, and the codes and statutes they set up became the precedents for all future mining camps throughout the West. California laws were copied by most of the new western states.

Not all the men who came to California worked in the gold fields. By the latter part of 1852, California's population was close to 250,000. Yet the actual number of miners was never that large. About 100,000 were mining and digging for gold; the rest were engaged in supplying or servicing those in the diggings, and many of them made more money than the hard-working miners.

More gold was found in 1849 and in later years than in 1848; but there were fewer spectacular strikes, and fewer miners found large amounts of gold. As time went by, new inventions and methods of mining affected life in the gold fields. A revolutionary discovery was made in March 1853 when Edward H. Mattison, a Connecticut Yankee, and two of his fellow miners invented hydraulic mining. Using a canvas hose and a tapered nozzle of sheet iron, a forceful jet of water was turned on a bank of dirt. This crumbled the earth and sent it sliding down to the miners, who washed it through their Long Toms.

Much greater quantities of dirt could now be washed; one man in a day could accomplish the work of dozens of men working with picks and shovels to break apart the dirt. Whole hills were washed away, and the entire natural environment was destroyed and altered by the miners in their frantic search.

Hydraulic mining and other technical developments changed the nature of the industry entirely. Mining became big business, with absentee ownership, huge amounts of capital, and joint-stock companies. No longer could a single miner prospect successfully with his pick and shovel. The individual forty-niner became a hired worker, laboring for a large company rather than on his own claim. Instead of hoping to hit it rich, he worked for a daily wage of $3. Whatever gold he found was the property of his employer.

For most forty-niners, there wasn't a pot of gold at the end of the rainbow. The overall spirit of California was one of boom and bust, rapid growth and speculation. Gold and greed ruled everything. The spectacular growth of San Francisco reflected the paradox of the gold rush. Taylor, in describing the early days of San Francisco at night, drew a picture of it as a magic-lantern city:

The appearance of San Francisco at night from the water, is unlike anything I ever beheld. The houses are mostly made of canvas, which is made transparent by the lamps within, and transforms them in the darkness, to dwellings of solid light. Seated on the slopes of its three hills, the tents pitched among the chaparral to the very summits, it gleams like an amphitheater of fire. Here and there shine out brilliant points from the decoy lamps of the gaming-houses. The picture has in it some-

Hydraulic mining

thing unreal and fantastic; it impresses one like the cities of the magic lantern, which a motion of the hand can build or annihilate.

But it was also a city of mirages, of unreachable hopes of riches and comforts for most of the population and the transitory miners who crowded its streets. In place of wealth, they found poverty; rather than gold and ease, they collected sickness and hardship; looking for companionship and adventure, they discovered selfishness and loneliness. Bewildered, exhausted, defeated by the hard life in the mines and the even harder existence in town, they were dazzled and lured by the magic shimmer of lights and public buildings, but found no warmth or comfort in this glow. They felt adrift and cut off from home and mankind. San Francisco was a boom town, but many of the forty-niners, merchants, workers, and hanger-ons went bust and lost all they had.

The mud ruts and bottomless holes of San Francisco's streets did more than swallow the bales of materials, casks, and barrels thrown into them to make them solid. The dreams and hopes of the forty-niners also sank into the endless swamp of the magic-lantern city. The adventurers had done most of the work, but they didn't enrich themselves. Woods summed up the true story of San Francisco and the gold rush for most of the argonauts:

There is much sickness now in this city. Many come down sick from the mines. There is a heartless unconcern in the community generally to the sufferings and wants of the many who are dying wretched deaths in the midst of them. It may not, perhaps, be possible that it should be otherwise. Every man is too much occupied with his

A cartoonist's comment on the gold rush

own concerns to be able to search out objects of charity; and there are so many such cases constantly recurring, as to induce a feeling of indifference, the result of familiarity with the sufferings of others.

By 1855 the day of the individual miner was largely gone, and the era of the colorful and romantic forty-niner was part of the past. Most of the mining camps became empty shells as the miners drifted away. They were still looking for a new El Dorado.

Many of the miners were bitter. Times were changing rapidly, and they had not made their pile. Home and riches were as far away as ever. The new breed of miners in California were nothing like the comrades they had known. The familiar mining haunts were either ghost towns or heavily industrialized diggings. They longingly looked back to "The Days of '49"—"to my comrades, they all loved me well . . . and whatever the pinch would never flinch." This haunting song recalls their dreams, their disappointments, and all the unfulfilled promises with which they started out.

Days of '49

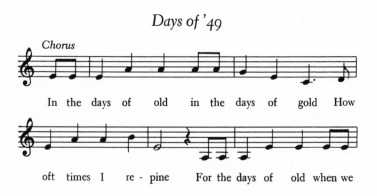

Chorus

In the days of old in the days of gold How

oft times I re - pine For the days of old when we

dug up the gold In the days of for - ty - nine.

I'm old Tom Moore from the bum-mer's shore, In the

good old gold - en days. They

call me a bum - mer and a gin - sot too, But

what care I for praise? I wan - der a - round from

town ___ to town, Just like a rov - ing

sign, And the peo - ple all say "There

goes Tom Moore of the days of for - ty - nine."

I'm old Tom Moore from the bummers, sure
In the good old golden days;
They call me a bummer and a ginsot, too,
But what care I for praise?
I wander around from town to town,
Just like a roving sign,
And the people all say, "There goes Tom Moore,
Of the days of '49."

My comrades, they all loved me well.
A jolly saucy crew,
A few hard cases I will admit,
Though they were brave and true.
Whatever the path they would never flinch,
They would never fret nor whine—
Like good old bricks, they stood the kicks,
In the days of '49.

There was Poker Bill, one of the boys,
Who was always in for a game;
Whether he lost or whether he won,
To him it was all the same.
He would ante up and draw his cards,
He'd go a hat full blind,
In the game with death Bill lost his breath,
In the days of '49.

There was old lame Jess, a hard old case,
Who never would repent;
He was never known to miss a meal,
Nor to ever spend a cent.
But old lame Jess, like all the rest,
To death did at last resign,
And in his bloom he went up the flume,
In the days of '49.

Of all the comrades that I've had,
There's none that's left to beast;
And I'm left alone in my misery
Like some poor wandering ghost.
And as I pass from town to town,
Just like some rambling sign,
"There goes Tom Moore, a bummer, sure,
Of the days of '49."

Return from El Dorado

SONG NOTES

California Boy is a variant of an old English love lament, *Sweet William,* that came to America during colonial days and was sung in Missouri, the starting point for the overland trip.

Banks of the Sacramento was a famous capstan shanty very popular among the seamen on the great clipper ships that made the run to California during the gold rush.

Blood-red Roses, a magnificent halyard shanty, was another favorite of seamen on the California run.

Sweet Betsey from Pike is one gold rush ditty that people in this country have never stopped singing. The author was a miner who styled himself "Old Put," and was perhaps the most talented of the gold rush songwriters. He borrowed the melody for *Sweet Betsey* from a traditional English folk song.

The Fools of '49 is another of Old Put's great songs. It tells of a race to California by land and sea that leads only to death.

Joe Bowers is one of the best-known of the goldmining songs. Its authorship is uncertain.

The Lousy Miner is one of Old Put's most famous songs, still being sung in the twentieth century.

The Miner's Dream, set to the charming minstrel tune, *Nelly Bly*, tells of one of the greatest misfortunes a person can experience—to remember in a time of wretchedness happy days that have vanished forever. This song, too, is by Old Put.

The Miners' Meeting is yet another of Old Put's songs. The melody to which he set it is a very old and famous traditional song, *The Bonny Boy*.

John Chinaman shows the bitter anti-Chinese prejudice of the white miners. It is set to an old Scottish tune, *John Anderson My Jo*.

The Dying Californian is a New England lament, based on a letter telling of a New Englander's death at sea on the way to California. The exquisite melody to which it is set was taken from a spiritual or hymn.

The Days of '49, composed when the gold rush was a thing of the past, looks back nostalgically to days gone by. Californians were still singing it well into the twentieth century.

BIBLIOGRAPHY

This bibliography has been designed for the reference of teachers, students, and school librarians. It includes the main sources used in the preparation of this book, and offers suggestions for further reading on the various topics. All works listed are in print at the time of writing (1976) unless otherwise stated.

General

A number of the journals and diaries of forty-niners are available to the modern reader, notably, Charles L. Camp, ed., *John Doble's Journal and Letters from the Mines* (Denver: The Old West Publishing Co., 1962); Alanzo Delano, *Life on the Plains and Among the Diggings* (1854. Reissued by University Microfilms, Ann Arbor, Michigan, 1966 and Arno Press, New York, 1973); William Kelly, Jr., *An Excursion to California Over the Prairies, Rocky Mountains and Great Sierra Nevada with a Stroll through the Diggings and Ranches of that Country* (1851. Reissued by Arno Press, New York, 1972); William Perkins, *Journal of Life at Sonora, 1849–52*, with an introduction and annotations by Dale L. Morgan and James R. Scobie (Berkeley: University of California Press, 1964); and Reuben Cole Shaw, *Across the Plains in '49*, edited with an introduction by Milo Milton Quaife (New York: Citadel Press, 1966).

Secondary accounts that present an overall view of the life of mining communities include Rodman W. Paul, *California Gold! The Beginning of Mining in the Far West* (Omaha, Nebraska: University of Nebraska Press, 1964), and the same author's *Mining Frontiers of the Far West, 1848–1880* (Albuquerque, New Mexico: University of New Mexico Press, 1963). John W. Caughey, *Gold Is the Cornerstone* (1948. Reissued under the title *The California Gold Rush* by the University of California Press, Berkeley, 1974, paperback), is a fine historical survey of the gold era. Hubert Howe Bancroft, *California Inter-Pocula* (Bancroft Press, 1967), deals with the varied social life and the activities of the forty-niners in the diggings, the mining towns, and San Francisco.

Robert F. Heizer and M. A. Whipple, eds., *The California Indians: A Source Book* (Berkeley: University of California Press, 1971, paperback) provides a thorough overview of the California aborigines. The songs of the forty-niners are reproduced in Richard E. Lingenfelter and Richard A. Dwyer, eds., *Songs of the American West* (Berkeley: University of California Press, 1968). A fine additional source by the same editors, *Songs of the Gold Rush* (Berkeley: University of California Press, 1965), is now out of print.

For the background of Jacksonian Democracy, of which the Gold Rush was a profound and dramatic expression, see Douglas T. Miller, *Then Was The Future: The North in the Age of Jackson* (New York: Alfred A. Knopf, Inc., 1974), and Ray Allen Billington, *The Far Western Frontier* (New York: Harper and Row, 1956, hardcover and paperback). The U.S. military victory over Mexico, which made the gold rush possible, is dealt with very effectively in Milton Meltzer, *Bound For the Rio Grande: The Mexican Struggle, 1845–50* (New York: Alfred A. Knopf Inc., 1974).

Gold Is Discovered in California
This chapter is based in part upon the works of Paul, Caughey, and Bancroft cited above. See also Hubert Howe Bancroft, *History of California*, Vol. IV (San Francisco, 1888. Reissued by Bancroft Press), and Jay Monaghan, *Australians and the Gold Rush: California and Down Under 1849–59* (Berkeley: University of California Press, 1966).

The News Spreads to the East
J. D. Borthwick, *The Gold Hunters* (1917. Reissued under the title *Three Years in California* by Biobooks, Oakland, California, 1948), tells how the excitement reached the East and set it aflame. Walker Wyman, ed., *California Emigrant Letters* (1952. Reissued by AMS Press, New York, 1972), contains dozens of letters from westward emigrants which were printed in eastern newspapers during the gold rush period.

Around Cape Horn or By Way of Panama to the Gold Fields
Oscar Lewis, *Sea Routes to the Gold Fields* (New York: Alfred A. Knopf, 1949), is a classic account of the trip around Cape Horn; now out of print, it may be found on many library shelves. For the Panama route, see John H. Kemble, *The Panama Route, 1848–69* (1943. Reissued by Da Capo Press, New York, 1972; also reprinted in *Publications in History*, vol. XXIX, Berkeley: University of California Press).

Overland by the California Trail
For the overland route along the California trail, see Reuben Cole Shaw, cited above; Dale L. Morgan, ed., *The Overland Diary of James Pritchard from Kentucky to California in 1849* (Denver, 1959); and Lorenzo D. Aldrich, *Journal of the Overland Route to California and the Gold Mines* (1851. Reissued by University Microfilms, Ann Arbor,

Michigan, 1966). Archer Butler Hulbert, *Forty-Niners: The Chronicle of the California Trail* (Boston: Little, Brown Co., 1931), is a composite account based on over 250 diaries, letters, and journals of the forty-niners, illustrated with hundreds of cartoons and contemporary drawings. Hulbert's book is out of print but still readily available on many library shelves. See also Charles F. McGlashan, *History of the Donner Party: A Tragedy of the Sierras* (1879. Revised edition edited by George H. Hinkle and Bliss M. Hinkle, Stanford University Press, Palo Alto, California, 1947. Reprint of 1879 edition reissued by University Microfilms, Ann Arbor, Michigan, 1966).

California Before the Gold Rush

For the native American peoples, see Heizer and Whipple, cited above, and the well-written introduction to the aboriginal Californians given in Chapter 15 of Alvin M. Josephy, Jr., *The Indian Heritage of America* (New York: Alfred A. Knopf Inc., hardcover and paperback, 1968). Alfred Robinson, *Life in California: A Historical Account of the Origins, Customs and Traditions of the Indians of Alta California* (1848. Reissued by Peregrine Smith, New York), contains excellent firsthand descriptions of the California Indians at the time of the gold rush. For the legends of these peoples see Theodora Kroeber, *The Inland Whale: Nine Stories Retold from California Indian Legends* (Berkeley: University of California Press, 1959).

For an interesting account of the impact of the gold rush upon the native Californians, see W. H. Hutchinson, *California, Two Centuries of Man, Land and Growth in the Golden State* (American West Publishing Co., 1969, Canfield Press, 1971, paperback). For Spanish California, see Pedro Fages, *A Historical, Political and Natural Description of California*, translated by Herbert I. Priestly (Ramona, California: Ballena Press, 1972). Richard H. Dana, *Two Years Before the Mast* (New York: E. P. Dutton, 1972, hardcover and paperback), is a classic account of Mexican life in early California along the Pacific coast. See also

William Robert Garner, *Letters from California*, edited by Donald Monro Craig (Berkeley: University of California Press, 1970).

Life in the Diggings and the Mining Camps

For accounts of life in the diggings, consult Daniel B. Woods, *Sixteen Months in the Diggings* (1851. Reissued by Arno Press, New York, 1973); Edward G. Buffum, *Six Months in the Gold Mines* (1850. Reissued by University Microfilms, Ann Arbor, Michigan, 1966); and William Shaw, *Golden Dreams and Waking Realities* (1851. Reissued by Arno Press, New York, 1973). Louise Amelia Clappe, *The Shirley Letters* (1849. Reissued by Peregrine Smith, New York, 1970, paperback), is the main primary source for a woman's view of life in the diggings. See also Dee Brown, *The Gentle Tamers: Women of the Wild West* (New York: Bantam Books, 1974, paperback), and Nancy Ross, *Westward the Women* (1974. Reissued by Ballantine, New York, paperback). Further information on the life, birth, and death of California mining towns is contained in Lambert F. Florin, *California Ghost Towns* (Seattle, Washington: Superior Publishers, 1971, paperback, and A. Ekman and others, *Old Mines and Ghost Camps of California*, edited by Edward E. Bartholomew (Frontier Books, 1968, paperback).

San Francisco

A fascinating study of daily life and special events in the growing city is Frank Soule, John Gibon, and James Nesbet, *The Annals of San Francisco* (1855. Reissued by Lewis Osborne, 1960). See also Bancroft, *History of California*, cited above, and Frank Marryat, *Mountains and Molehills, or, Recollections of a Burnt Journal* (Westport, Connecticut: Greenwood Press, 1975).

Pride and Prejudice

There are many sources of information about discrimination against foreign-born miners. See in particular: George E. Faugsted, Jr., *Chilenos in the California Gold Rush* (San

Francisco: R and E Research Associates); Elmer C. Sandmeyer, *The Anti-Chinese Movement in California* (Urbana: University of Illinois Press, 1973, hardcover and paperback); Stuart C. Miller, *The Unwelcome Immigrant: The American Image of the Chinese 1785–1882* (Berkeley: University of California Press, 1969, hardcover and paperback); Kenneth G. Goode, *California's Black Pioneers: A Brief Historical Survey* (Chicago, Illinois: Rand McNally & Co., 1974, paperback); Matt S. Meier and Feliciano Rivera, *The Chicanos: A History of Mexican Americans* (New York: Hill and Wang, 1972, hardcover and paperback); and Roger Daniels and Spencer C. Olin, Jr., eds., *Racism in California: A Reader in the History of Oppression* (New York: Macmillan Co., 1972, paperback).

The Extermination of the California Indians

The clearest, best written, and most stirring account of the extermination of the California Indians is Theodora Kroeber, *Ishi in Two Worlds: A Biography of the Last Wild Indian in North America* (Berkeley: University of California Press, 1961, hardcover and paperback). The author devotes the first half of her book to the hunting down and slaughter of the California Indians. Kroeber's *Ishi: Last of His Tribe* (New York: Bantam Books, 1973, paperback) is a classic reconstruction of Ishi's experience based upon the author's own knowledge of the man. For the general context of the California Indian tragedy, consult J. P. Dunn, *Massacres of the Mountains: A History of the Indian Wars of the Far West 1815–75* (1886. Reissued by Archer House Inc., New York).

ACKNOWLEDGMENTS

Thanks to my editor and friend, Tony Scott, for his help, encouragement, and guidance in the preparation of this book, and for the care he took in preparing all the music for the songs. Thanks go to Frances Foster for her aid in guiding me to a conclusion of this manuscript and for her knowledge in moving things along and pulling everything together. I'd especially like to thank my wife, Marion Nesler Seidman, for her perceptive reading and critique of each chapter as it emerged from the typewriter. Her encouragement and faith helped to bring the story of the forty-niners to fruition. Lastly, to my children, who are convinced that Father can do anything—and their conviction is contagious. I caught it myself.

Grateful acknowledgment is made for the use of illustrations:

New York Public Library, Picture Collection, *frontis*, 33, 46, 52, 64, 120, 131, 132, 178, 209; I. N. Phelps Stokes Collection, 158;

Library of Congress, 13;

New-York Historical Society, 14, 35, 60–61 (formerly in the collection of Thomas Streeter), 107, 129, 141, 152, 155, 160, 163, 175, 181, 211, 216–17 (formerly in the collection of Thomas Streeter);

Museums at Stony Brook, Long Island, 25;

American Antiquarian Society, 40;

Huntington Library, San Marino, California, 76–77, 90–91, 105;

California State Library, Sacramento, 122;

Lowie Museum of Anthropology, University of California, Berkeley, 201.

The maps on pages 49, 73, 100, and 126 are by Ed Malsberg.

INDEX

Alta, Calif., 94
American Encyclopedia, 15
American miners, 117, 119, 134
American River, 5, 11, 177
American Valley, 144
Anderson, Robert A., 199
Angelique (ship), 38
Atlantic Ocean, 56, 59, 62
Austria, 26
"Ayer's Pain Killer," 84

Baja, Calif., 110
Ballou, Mary B., quoted, 162–164
Baltimore, Md., 26, 31
Baltimore Sun, 21
Bancroft, Hubert, quoted, 10, 53, 58, 63, 65, 116, 128, 157, 189, 191
"Banks of the Sacramento, The" (song), 27, 29–31
Beale, Edward Fitzgerald, 21
Blacks, 66, 182–183
"Blood-Red Roses" (song), 68–69
Bohemia, 26
Borthwick, J. D., quoted, 125, 140, 154–156, 173
Boston, Mass., 26, 31, 99, 113, 114, 115

Botas, 115
Brannan, Sam, 5, 18
Browne, J. Ross, quoted, 195, 196–197
Bruff, Joseph Goldborough, 71–72, 74–77, 83, 84, 86–87, 90–91, 105
Buchanan, James, 20
Buffalo, 70, 86, 87
Buffam, Edward G., quoted, 103, 104–106, 174–176
Bureau of Indian Affairs, 196
Burnett, Peter H., quoted, 192

California: admitted to the union, 182; climate, 101; gold discovered in, 3, 20; industries, 114–118; legislation in, 182–183, 192–193, 207; physical description of, 99, 101; Spanish colonization of, 110–111
California, University of, 198, 199
California (steamship), 65
California and the Way to Get There (Sherwood), 43
"California Boy" (song), 19
California Indians, see Indians of California
California Legislature, 192–193

LAURENCE I. SEIDMAN has a special interest in the legend and lore of the American West and is the author of *Once In the Saddle: The Cowboy's Frontier,* also in The Living History Library. An historian and folklorist, he is an authority on the use of folk songs and folklore in teaching social studies to children. He has been an elementary school teacher and is now a professor at C. W. Post College. He lives with his family in Great Neck, New York.

JOHN ANTHONY SCOTT is the general editor of The Living History Library and the author of three of its books: *Hard Trials on My Way, Settlers on the Eastern Shore,* and *Trumpet of a Prophecy.* He teaches American Studies at both high school and university levels.